One Hundred Poems

Robert Klein Engler

Alphabeta Press
CHICAGO

Printed by Alphabeta Press
CHICAGO

ISBN-0-944300-11-1

email: alphabpres@aol.com

Made in the United Sates of America

Poi si rivolse, e parve di coloro
che corrono a Verona ilo drappo verde
per la campagna: e parve di costoro

quelli che vince, non colui che perde.

— Dante

Printed in the USA by

MORRIS PUBLISHING

3212 East Highway 30 • Kearney, NE 68847 • 1-800-650-7888

Contents

Acknowledgments

"Holding On" first appeared in *Opus*. • "Six Jesuit Priests Were Tortured and Killed in El Salvador" first appeared in *The International Poetry Review* • "How to Draw a Picture of a Naked Man" first appeared in *Off the Rocks* • "Shipwrecked on the North Atlantic" first appeared in *Bluff City*. • "Two Lines in Shakespeare That Mean the Same Thing" first appeared in *Christopher Street* • "Life Is Raw, Art Is Cooked" first appeared in *Widner Review* • "Fragments of Sappho, Filled In" first appeared in *Queer Planet Review* • "Two Men Lived a Long Time Together Here" and "If Nature Puts a Burden on a Man" first appeared in *Lucky Star* • "Walking by the Moon" first appeared in *Green River Review* • "The Perfect Flower of Human Time" first appeared in *South Dakota Review* • "Morning Train Through Allentown" first appeared in *Anvil* • "Serenade for Elvis Presley" first appeared in *Yellow Door* • "The Colosseum in Ruins" "Fire at the Old Factory" "Icehouse" and "Flower Festival at Genzano" first appeared in *Whetstone* • "Epithalamium" first appeared in *The Windless Orchard* • "I Have Read Out the Gold Upon the Wall" "Letter to Brainsure" and "St. Joseph's Church, Stratford" first appeared in *A.U. Review* • "Sleepers" first appeared in *Intrinsic* • "Cold April at the Des Moines Art Museum" first appeared in *Tantalus Poetry Review* • "Voodoos and Don'ts" first appeared in *Hyphen* • "Perfectly Normal" first appeared in *Lip Service* • "The Greeks Had a Terrible Fire Too" first appeared in *Manhattan Poetry Review* • "Thirteen" first appeared in *Northward Journal* • "Sigüenza" first appeared in *Poet Lore* • "Cartagena" first appeared in *Cadence* • "Sorting the Flames" first appeared in *Where Men Gather* • "Driving Home from the Bistro" first appeared in *Seams* • "Flesh" first appeared in *Hammers* • "San Francisco Fortunes" first appeared in *QRHYME* • "Slow Sunday" first appeared in *Waves* • "Winter Solstice" first appeared in *Poetry Canada Review* • "The Drive from Work" first appeared in *Arts Alive* • "The Scar on the Hand of the Porno Star" first appeared in *Voices Against the Wilderness* • "From Dust to Dust" first appeared in the *Dalhousie Review* • "A Descent to Darkness on Extended Wings" first appeared in *California State Poetry Quarterly* • "All Saints Day" first appeared in *Sidewalks* • "Remembering Aschenbach" first appeared in *Porch* • "Resurrection" first appeared in *Christianity and the Arts Magazine* • "Summer Solstice" "At the Beach" "Marble Statues of a Kouros" "Young Sophocles Leading the Victory Chorus" and "Coda" first appeared in *Tomorrow Magazine* • "Could the Heart At Ease Still Love, Or Is that Ease Being in Love?" first appeared in *The Neovictorian* • "To All the Heterosexuals Whose Lives Are Heavy as Stone" first appeared in *This* • "Postcard" first appeared in *Laughing Boy Review* • "Conundrum" first appeared in *Fish Stories Collective 3* • "Old Movies" first appeared in *Zone 3* • "Still Life With Sunrise" first appeared in *Hyphen* • "Three Poems for Kabbalah" first appeared in *Fish Stories*. • "Crisscrossed Names" first appeared in *Ebbing Tide* • "Homework" first appeared in

Real Poetik • "Poor Apology" first appeared in *Tendril* • "Overnight by English Bay" first appeared in *Waves* • "Dim Conjunctions" first appeared in *Webster Review* • "Conversation" first appeared in *Somewhere Else to Publish* • "Hands" first appeared in *Four Quarters* • "Mozart and the Use of Light to Capture Loneliness" first appeared in *Nightsun* • "The Highway" first appeared in *Hyphen* • "After Scotch and Soda" first appeared in the *Thunder Egg* • "In Memory of All the Homosexuals Cut in Half by Saws" first appeared in *Tribe* • "The Difference Between Then and Now is That Then They Believed in Revolution" first appeared in *The Chicago Literary Review* • "Summer Threnody" first appeared in *Farmer's Market* • "Pawn Shop" first appeared in *Plainsong* • "Imagined, While in Traffic, A Cold Spring" first appeared in *The Kentucky Poetry Review* • "The Melons" first appeared in The *Willow Review* • "Illusions" first appeared in *Seams* • "North by the River" first appeared in *The Critic* • "The Velvet Cord" first appeared in *The Windless Orchard* • "Why We Don't Have a Statue of Goethe in the Corner Park" first appeared in *The Rockford Review* • "Sunset at the Cloister" first appeared in *Cedar Rock* • "Planting Tulips" first appeared in *Poet Lore* • "The Sun Catcher" first appeared in *Culebra* .

One Hundred Poems

Song at Twilight

Lie down beside me, remember how it was:
laughing, we counted the leaves as they fell
to the Commons; pull me closer, because

the earth pulls closer the falling light and does
not worry over who is ill or well.
Wrap you arms around me, hush the gauze

of rain at Wellfleet Harbor—what does
rain know about the language of farewell —
our only blanket was speech, and that was

a threadbare cover for our hearts—because
I wanted you too much, and you, well,
having to get back, drove non-stop, it was

a wonder, our car overheating, the buzz
of tires, silence building a white shell
around our hearts; that is what distance does.

Like the tedium of an ant, our journey was
a deed so small the world could hardly tell—
wrap you arms around me, slow time's buzz,
don't be afraid to remember how it was.

Holding On

The campus trees are red and gold.
I see him walk from his math class
to his car, off to tennis,
bouncing a ball, swinging his gym bag.
I guess he knows he is beautiful.

What is that glory, but another apple of life?
More will be made next season.
The black ducks by the pond, bending
their necks like question marks,
know this, and yet do not know it.

What they hold on to is what they know.
Today, it is light so brittle you'd think
the sun would shatter if it were to move.
This is all anyone can hold of beauty,
our lashes beat back the rest.

What did my father hold?
A dilapidated house or two, some tools,
my mother's soft shoulders in the dark,
and then he was off, a hole in his heart,
falling down into questions.

The silver, wordless opening of the pond
is more like a mirror now, but the ducks
know it has another echo, an echo
that beats like the bouncing of a ball, imagine
the abundance of not wanting anything at all.

A Traveler Returns

In one corner, a queen still holds court,
and along the bar, the same young men,
or are they the illusion of young men,
pose and posture, wait for something to say,
and spread their Levied legs like a harbor.
Where there was wood, there is now glitter.
I think he sat on that stool. I was on the next.
We talked for hours, but not one word
about the apartment we used to share.
When I left him there, I said to myself,
Be strong. Months later he was dead.
Above me, twin balls of mirrors slowly spin,
a relentless milling, like orbits in syrup,
and on the dance floor below, falling,
revolving, are cloven footprints of light.

Six Jesuit Priests Were Tortured
and Killed in El Salvador

We see thirty seconds of it on the TV news —
six bloody bodies sprawl face down in a field.
They cover them with white sheets, voices
in the background mumble Spanish while
an anchorman fills in vague details about
liberation theology, death squads, then cuts
to a recorded interview with one of them
shot six months earlier, middle-aged, bearded,
vibrant, dressed like a worker, who talks
of social justice, sharing the wealth, peace.
It is a resurrection of the dead by video.

The Bishop of El Salvador, ironic land,
carrying the savior's name, with his red skull
cap, blesses the bodies and condemns the deed.
"Thy Kingdom come, Thy will be done."
Men of God accused of being communists,
babies without milk, bananas, the landed
gentry riding to their latifundia in polished
sedans, and to the North, ordinary people,
deliberately indifferent to the problem —
"Look, I got my own life to worry about."

On TV we see a road by a gas station,
the humid air presses down like hands
of ordination, a reporter speaks into a black
microphone, in the distance a column of oily
smoke rises, a motor scooter whirs by,
the guerrillas press their offensive by daylight,
life goes on, men clean their rifles, up all night,
they can't sleep the sleep of the exhausted.
"Did you see the blood when I cut off his balls?"
God's work takes so much out of you.

How to Draw a Picture of a Naked Man

For Phil Luing

1

Imagine snow falling,
softening a faint outline of earth—
down there, worms are busy on a profile.

2

When he was a boy, his mother
caught him drawing pictures
of naked men —"Never," she said,
"draw a man the way he really is."

3

"I am sorry," he says to the priest
listening in the charcoal darkness,
"But as long as I'm in this body,
I'll be back."

4

Two attempts this week
to draw his face from memory —
the failures at surgery lay crumpled—
don't cut, unless you have a steady hand.

5

His brush moves over paper
like wind over a landscape of snow.
In winter, the most used path
is slipperiest.

6

Remember, how warm was
the inkwell of his mouth —
you make the dot of light
in the eye with an erasure.

7

Still nothing—he listens
to Brahms on the stereo —
"In the room the women come and go
talking of Michelangelo."

8

Lao-tzu and K'ung Fu-tse meet by a waterfall.
Do not go to China to study the nude.

9

Look how he renders
the muscles of the chest
with just the right blush of pastel —
trouble is, we don't kiss with our eyes.

10

"Twenty-eight young men bathe by the shore,
twenty-eight young men and all so friendly ... ."
Keep your pencil sharp!

11

A question spreads over his mind
like wide light over a field —
does his drawing have Buddha nature?

12

That is it —
just line and shade —
nothing solid in the darkness.
Never draw what you love
too much.

13

"It was snowing
and it was going to snow —"
ice to paper, blood to ink,
bones to brushes.
We burn, and burn again.

Shipwrecked on the North Atlantic —
The First of February, 1826

I

The storm tosses us like a straw.
Our sails blow out.
Carpenters saw down the masts.
With my eyes shut, the ship slams against
the waves like a barn door loose in the wind.
Afterwards, the deck is a mystery of wires
and tangled lines—we drift for days —
it is like looking into oil —
there is the smell of tar and old fish.

II

You don't know what thirst is.
The soul shrinks, the tongue swells
to the size of a second body.
The taste of salt makes us mad.
Those who drink the sea will die.

III

Hunger grows like a wild vine.
Even our toes have teeth.
We chew on our belts and shoes.
I look at the men and see wolves.

IV

When the first man dies
we slit his throat and drink the blood.
It was thick and warm —
custard with a taste of iron.
Someone cuts off the head and hands
and throws them into the sea.
We butcher the body and set strips of meat
on the quarterdeck to cure in the sun.
This is our food—we drift for days on end.

V

When my fiancé dies I drink his blood too.
His strips of flesh sweeten like licorice
on the sun-bleached deck.
Finally we see a sail —
the HMS Blonde sends over a boat.
A lieutenant is shocked to see us,
so worn, but signals his captain,
"They have yet plenty of fresh meat."

VI

I live in London now
and keep a sponge damp
for pressing to my lips.
I never married.
When the fog comes
I light a fire and stay inside.
Just the smell of stew makes me sick.
Do you think the city has enough food?

Two Lines in Shakespeare That Say the Same Thing

Earl cooks sausage in the kitchen.
Around the front room chairs are posted
like wagons in a circle—we listen
to poetry above the knock of pans.
The sausage frying sounds like rain falling.

Larry reads his poem about swimmers.
They are far away and he cannot make out
what they really look like, just ordinary men
jumping into the water from a small boat.
Barry says he should take a comb and run it
through the text to get out the loose words.

What would Gregg say about this botched
work? Many things besides poems start well
and end badly—situations we don't expect,
like the one Larry writes about where he saw
from behind this boy with fine hair
and delicate, artist's hands, sitting

at a coffeehouse table, writing, no doubt,
poems in his most certainly sensitive journal.
From behind he was all we dream about.
Larry had to see it whole, so he gets up,
as if to take a pee, and walks by to look —
unaware, he reads right past the ending—
"I was disappointed you were not beautiful."

Life is Raw, Art is Cooked

As we leave the ballet,
two street people beg on the corner
with plastic cups from Burger King.
"What is the wider truth of pain?"
I ask myself as we walk under the hot lights
of the theater marquee, "Can art make
such a leap that we leave the particulars
of our own life and see what unites us,
or is there just this life, self-contained,
her life next to me, the men begging,
each with their own destiny, a corps de ballet,
all dancing and laughing and glittering,
all of us in our particular light?"
"You can receive light from anyone,"
she said to me earlier over drinks—
echoing California, she added,
"I'm waiting for mine to come."
"Not only am I waiting, the dead are waiting too,"
I thought to say to the maraschino cherry
sticking out of my glass like a microphone.
When that man sitting next to me at the ballet
pushed his leg against mine, and I felt the hot
music of his thigh in the dark cavern of the theater,
I thought for a moment it was true,
there is another world more real than this one
on the street, but the lights went up
and the applause drowned us in a flapping
of feathers, a rattle that sounded like rain.
Now the sound of holiday bells,
the ring of nickels in a plastic cup,
slow, faint beats of overcoated hearts
drift off into the night—we walk side by side
alone, a promenade of strangers
breathing the foggy breath of crowds
back into a raw, white air.

Fragments of Sappho, Filled In

they come and they go,
like fireflies over a summer meadow,
we see their light, for a moment,
then wonder where they are ...

... and on smooth, downy beds
of cotton you released desire like a bird ...
it flew away with a soft clapping ...

my dear, it's all right,
we were young then, like a chick
who is hungry and will eat a pebble,
what did you know?

... and I, well, I see now, love
like paralysis or kidney stones,
is something that happens ...

like the blushing apple the apple pickers
surrender to the tip of the branch top
you were impossible to reach
even with a stick...

... and no one else whispered ...
nothing sacred would stop us ... rain
came ... we could not hold back ...

Two Men Lived A Long Time Together Here

I'm thinking about what he said,
how when all the books are closed,
the foundation of the heart is memory.
This comes to me while the cancer of autumn
advances through the birch and maple groves.
I remember how he and Wheeler lived
in a center of calm behind that row of trees.
We used to talk by the pond when it was clean
as ice. Now it's filled with water moss.
We studied pockets of mist in the low grass,
saw fog wrap the hills, even when
a September sun blazed past ten o'clock.
I remember, there was a field of crickets
here a month ago too. Now they are the mold
of next's year's dandelions and goldenrod.
It's expected, this being a place of seasons,
a place where punk-weeds are fat as cigars,
or the perfume of fresh-mowed roadside grass
bites the air once or twice a year. For now,
we hang Indian corn and cut pumpkins
with one-tooth smiles, give them candles for eyes,
remembering the color of a coffin resembles
sunlight brass upon the chestnut leaves.

In the field boys are playing football
to the whistle and shout of coach Williams.
Their helmets make them seem stellar forms
of life, with large heads and childish limbs.
I like to imagine what will come from
their couplings, who, in the years to come,
will take their love, how this innocence
will find its root in generations,
how out of this game of discipline will come
their bodies mannered in the ways of men.
Could it be possible, I wonder,
as a wobbling pass arches through the air,
that the human soul may find another form?

Something equal to our hope, a suitable form,
protected, like the football-playing boys, from bump
and cut, fitted for the sport of immortality.
Then we would not go sick, but share wine
with our lovers, cut flowers, listen to the seasons
play fingers with the willows by the pond.

There is a hint of this in animals, I think.
Just now a cat is walking its profile across
a fence on its way to some feline business.
I can't help think how it reminds me
of the embodiment of human attributes,
but without the identity and particulars of names.
All nature seems species, a kind of remembering,
the way God would remember if he lost a lover.
The black crows stealing their way to winter,
sweat bees busy in the late sun, all have a rhythm
less than love demands: the beat of wings,
a breath of wind, the wink of stars,
and all of this here, an arch of light over
the trees, a road curving to gravel sides,
the darkening of blue in the bowl of the sky,
all of it, in its substantial reality, is as if it were
a remembrance of another place.
Even the hum of power mower and home saw
from behind the trees that tells me Ronnie Sims
has come up from town to help old man Wheeler
ready for winter is moving off somewhere else.
He's better now, after the funeral, out cutting
grass, the last roses, pyramids of firewood.

Walking by the Moon

There is a limit at the end
of form where great and small
share a secret edge, where mystery
turns upon itself. Perhaps you

know it in the faint and friction
sound of slippers sliding in a
ballet blanc, or find it rests
upon the atoms of a tongue from

which the world of rhyme speaks
out. It is as small as all the
parts that glue space, as razor
as an edge where rests smallest

of the small. Here the world
bursts. A hinge on it is turned
and earth and sun and galaxies
shine far beyond the limit of

our scope. More high and wide
than firmament it goes, to ether
and the largest of the large.
It is the limit and the end of

it, the limit found when walking
by the moon, or writing words,
or making love to phantom eyes
so ever large and small.

The Perfect Flower of Human Time

*Marriage has many pains, but celibacy
has no pleasures.*

—*Samuel Johnson*

"The letter comes, ten years late, but
it comes and I am ready for my part,
ready to accept his calculations
with calculations of my own.
Ten years, half of it on a couch,
and he would ask me to unfold the layers
of my skirt and admit him to the darkness
where calculations can effect a birth.
I am ripe by these words, this letter
asking me to start again, to rise from
my salon leisure and edit manuscripts,
to be bride and run a house this late date,
to be a mother when mothering has no means,
to accept all his smoke close to me,
inside, weak as I am, enough for one.

"He writes because he finally comes to the end
of desire, because his days are pressed
upon by common thoughts.
He would walk some common meanings
from those long and sculptured legs.
I know the doubt, the inability to figure
how else to live when the only love we did not
calculate is dead, what else to do, where
else to go outside of domesticity?
I know, Alfred, the long, unnatural grief,
the truth and trial of unnatural power,
how the world of men and women immune to love
eats at your heart like a beetle on a rose;
the horror of its iridescent, insect
skin, mouthing velvet, sucking
the blood of nature's fairest flower.
I know, Alfred, your move to me is

cradled and considerate, after such dry years
you can only say what you mean in verse,
living something else—your art is true,
your actions, they alone are bent
to make the world aware that poetry
is written out but never lived —
not in this world, not in the world
of clubs and carriages, parlors
and potted plants, polite conversation,
not the way a poet laureate must instruct
the young, not the way a queen admits
to memory her favorite verse ...
O, Alfred, what else can I do? Of course
I'll take your offer to heart,
edit your desire as best I can,
hope by spelling out your lines
I come to share the secret of the hand
that would hold mine, yet wished to hold
much more the crafted head
of Cambridge's perfect flower.
Yes, Alfred, if Hallam only knew,
I will be the bride."

The Days Assemble

The world of captive beasts is blind.
For these the days assemble as old misers
thumbing dumb gold, for these
time is creased and stored, put away
like table linen on a shelf.
"There is enough training,"
wild things cry, "Enough preparation,
when will we see what we must take?"

It is another dim, English day.
Like a falcon trained on leather gloves,
his beak polished with bone, feathers oiled,
he sets out to search the bookstalls.
Shall he finger his way across some poet's
Braille, does the moisture in the sky
discourage the sparrows?

Soon, when the air is dry,
the flocks will migrate.
Then, the outlines of his eyes
will be touched, then
he is pointed to the promise
and let fly.
He leaves his leather rest
to throw his talons at the sky.

Morning Train through Allentown

For Bill Beattie

Horses gather by a stream to drink.
Some cows lie upon the morning grass
to dream away the lazy hours
that pass these misty Pennsylvania hills.

Nearby a gentle slope, fenced black
with sapling trees, contains the spotted
graves of those who hold their final pose
meters from the railroad track.

As Chris and I get off to gather this and that,
I imagine how our mortal past, the milky
matter of our parts, like mist, is all
too easily dispatched by light.

And so I offer, Bill, a traveler's prayer,
that light will also lift the dead to live again,
and though this simple hope is sent for you,
it prays the unknown too abide.

Serenade for Elvis Presley

The dark underbellies
of evening clouds wind by.
They bring down from the Yukon
a hint of wilderness.
Half summer, half Canada,
the weather inches southward,
while cool nights and dry pigments
ache to paint the harvest.
Hidden by ritual camouflage
the small field insects
begin to crawl back to dust.
All that is rare or persistent
in us creeps in a summer
dream and is exhausted.
It is like the temporary fragment
of white on the willow branches at dawn.

While the moth tunnels the corner
or under the lip of a shelf,
I think of putting things away,
and how the recent dead are put away.
We seal them in oak or brass,
elsewhere, naked children
poke at bone or ash.
But they too are put away,
and on and on,

like those dolls from Russia
that fit one inside the other,
usually making a family.

Parceled to the past,
we put our parents away.
Over this storage the seasons roll
like a Venetian canopy.
Beneath this shell of taffeta
you wake one day with a pain.

Bottles take their place
on the bedside table,
the house grows old with odor,
a box is measured for satin
and kindlewood struck.
Now the dark bottom of the sky
prepares an embassy for night,
unlocks the lids on ice.

The Colosseum in Ruins

Not much of the building stands now,
just part of the front wall and an arch
facing Wabash—a sign says, "Keep Out."

There is a turret, some fractured ramparts
and skeleton doors with their green paint
echoing, cottonwood, milkweed, thistle.

My mother, reminiscing, told me this
was the great hall of her youth, together
with her lost sisters she would walk

its block-long length, wait for the shows
and spectacles that would thrill their
innocence—the circus, six-day bike races,

dancing—they believed it, like childhood,
was indestructible—but Pearl died at eighteen
from pneumonia, and Mabel after that.

You could be overwhelmed by the panorama
of shades and forlorn lives that swarm
in the grass here, transparent films

of another time that whistle as they move.
Is this what comes of us, bald block of ruins,
grass growing from a drain like hair

from an old man's ear, toothless portals,
the busy buzz of another world of radios
and glass, revolving round a shell, paralyzed

like a sore widow half asleep at noon?
Cannot the eye of imagination, that sees all,
leaf through the panels of our past

and recognize how an orphan and her
sisters walked home to a wooden flat,
laughing again at the adventure

they had under these vaults of tar?
See, their wool dresses turn away the rain,
and small hats of straw with silk flowers

do them well in the eyes of boys
who dream of black cars
and shine their shoes with the paste

of expectation, look down, all-seeing eye,
and remember the place from where each
stone falls, each hair, each word —

let some memory stay indestructible,
so that when she returns she will recognize
her street and the wind calling her name.

I Have Read Out the Gold upon the Wall

That which you love well remains.

—*Ezra Pound*

The great beast of irony that terrorizes
the pagan generations of our age
ends with eating its own children.
The great fetters of irony that run
from Freud to Nixon's Christmas bombing,
that even now embrace punk rock creeps
shouting, "Ezra, Ezra, Ezra Pound,
walking up and walking down,"
bind us to the lingam of despair.

Once upon a time, symbols fell to the earth
from an imagination beyond the sky—roses,
profiles, Roman moons, the iris and the acorn.
When Greeks grew mortal from the earth,
marble and medallions worked for men.

Now so much specific rendering makes us mad.
Can you imagine—someone leaves a continent
of Philistines to write poetry—and the irony —
the Philistines award him the prize Bollingen.
Someday I'm going to check into a motel
and sign my name, "Hugh Selwyn Mauberly."
No one even looks up.

Sleepers

Some nights he'd turn from his wife
and stare beyond the bedroom walls.
She sleeps embraced, content with life.

Almost annoyed, he feels her warm
rump in his back, joined to him
like a Siamese opposite—her arms

enfolding the night. From a window
the breeze fills her simple sleep,
carries him to another love, long ago,

to the North country, another season.
Beyond the palms and sand, someone
waits, weighs alone the parted reasons,

and calls from sleep a breathless call.
Some nights he turns from his wife
and listens blank beside the wall.

Cold April at the Des Moines Art Museum

For Christopher Craven

All the way here the red roads
of Iowa unwind in the rain.
Then, a bronze man, naked,
standing guard before one
white room after another.

Next to the deep loneliness
of beauty, the season opens
like a letter, unfolds
the petals of flowers
that bloom regardless.

In the garden, rose bushes
are tied up, a fir tree
stands with dripping arms
like a ballet dancer
dropping sleeves of moss.

Off somewhere, in another forest,
an archer waits silent as snow.
He does not worry how to live.
For him, his art is his bow.
Make every poem an arrow.

Voodoos and Don'ts

Tonight on the TV news the anchorman said
scientists have discovered it's a difference in the brain.
The doubt, the pulling back from fire, an empty bed,
don't worry, they are all now so easy to explain.

I sit in a bar and drink, listening to little worlds
unravel like string—in the next room a man plays
piano and sings show tunes, "What good is sitting
alone in your room?" The great expanse of days,

years hazy on the horizon, roll past my eyes
as if I were on a train, seeing, but unable to touch.
They know now, I say to myself, it's the brain,
they cut open twenty skulls and looked inside.

Like toy guns, flags popped out, they had "Gay"
written on them, and the scientists were content.
That's why, back then, he smiled and I fell for it,
not knowing it was just chemicals or a current

running through the skull like a blood, blue river,
or maybe it was just grains of sand—I twirl
a plastic toothpick—so what, there's no going over,
like an oyster, you feel an itch and turn it to a pearl.

Perfectly Normal

Deliverance motors into the harbor.
A gray-green water laps
against the columns of the pier
with the gurgle of a slow fountain.
The wind retreats now to rest
for blowing in the winter.
Goodbye to the sails of summer.

What is this going away
and coming back, simply a dream,
or a shuttle on the loom of sleep?
When you said goodbye, you came
back only in my memory,
a ghost ship, mast fingering the fog,
out of season, with bells for eyes.

The Greeks Had a Terrible Fire Too

There are two ways of going through —
the way of fire and the way of water.
There is also the memory of a visionary
marvel, when in high school chemistry,
Mr. Vandenberg dropped a bit of phosphorus
in a pan of water—burning water!
Our youth imagined a city of phosphorus
on a rainy day, the heat of fire storms,
each drop a spark and smoke, the world
wet with fire. There are two ways,
the burning up and the drowning,
and then there is being in between —
burning water, drowning fire.

Now is the quiet breath after breakfast.
The last warm day in October slips
its south light through the glass doors.
Motes are dancing in sunbeams, blue
plates are stacked by the sink, brown coffee
and cigarette ash ring and dot the table wood.
Those last words he said, "I'll call,
for sure," circle like smoke in the sun.

The Greeks had a terrible fire too.
They hurled it at the ships of their enemies.
But all Sparta would be amazed if I came
back and struck a match, lit a fire by one
stroke. Yet there would be an old man,
I'm sure, who would see this and say nothing.
He would limp back to his white walls
and remember Archidamus,
ripe son of the hero Leonidas,
remember the hot August when Archidamus
stopped by his open door for a drink.

Thirteen

One February day
with fog and dampness everywhere,
a humid southwest winter wind
begins to thaw the city square.

From mullioned windows of an attic room
a boy observes the seasons come and go.
He spends an hour of emptiness
that those without a father know.

The sky is tilting into spring
and snows are melting down to gray.
The ways of childhood are carried off
like ice upon the river wide away.

From his window seat he scouts the world
with every effort of his eye,
while dreaming still the other place
that left him here to spy.

Sigüenza

It is cool
deep in the cave
cathedrals of Castile.

Outside —
the flame blue sky —
white walls

with geraniums —
jars of water.
Here the cold stone

is like a salve.
While men walk on the moon
the brown saints no longer thirst —

their robes empty of flesh
except for hands and face.
They dream what the paralyzed

dream
not walking
but floating place to place —

enduring
not the centuries
but day to day.

Cartagena

A breath off autumn's red lips
Awakes the ripe, ridged world —
Tempting rusted leaves, wave after wave,
To run on the raptured tongues of wind —
Tempting the sky to glide the geese back
Before shutting her ivory splashed mouth —
Tempting me through humid caves
To taste again his kiss.

Sorting the Flames

The archaeologist of night
works with moon shards.
I press quicksilver
between glass, collect shadows
from the corners of the old house,
sort and store the fossil sparks.

My father comes down the hall
heading for the bathroom.
He just left my mother.
All oil and hair,
like some fabled Noah.
He tells me to get back to bed.
I have seen his nakedness
and it is an abomination.
In the glow of the old house,
in the hall that seemed
magisterial in length,
in the light of childhood,
I see my dead father.

It is his face I see now
in the glass of the mirror.
Mother and I watch his eyes.
They trace the darkness back
to where I was called from nothing.
His hands sort the flames.

Driving Home from the Bistro

A cold winter moon
comes full and round
through the thorn woods.
Blue-white balloon
floating up from sheets of snow.

"Let us catch it," cry the trees.
The knuckle and branch of their
old fingers, arthritic in the wind,
scrape against the sky,
scatter grains of stars.

From my bed I see the winter moon
cold and bright in the west.
A snow-blue shaft of light
stripes the floor,
glows upon the sheets like radium.

It is the same moon that spelled
magic when I walked late to my car,
ice steps scattering beneath
my feet like stones —
your taste of salt still on my lips.

Flesh

We are crafted for coupling
tuned to touch —
finger woven with finger,
leg over leg,
flesh smooth as a fig,
warm breath of night.

Even the great whale
that sings in the sea
can only slide in love,
or do it
like mysterious birds,
mating while they arch
above the chimneys.

Could the crusted ant kiss,
surely it would,
or the noble horse lie
with its lover
or the faithful dog
whisper a poem,
surely they would.

We are crafted for coupling,
tuned to touch.
Holding you close asleep,
I tell you this,
flesh sweet as a fig,
slow breath of morning.

San Francisco Fortunes

Light fades from the transom.
A dark shield of long shadows
files across the lawn.
Asleep, he sprawls half naked
on the hotel bed.

In the dull light
his face presses the pillow
like a fish on ice in Chinatown.
The eyes that were Australian deep
are now dim, concluded disks.

As light moves to lower latitudes,
the winds change. I hold my breath.
"He's tired of me," I think.
Anxious, I wait the tide of shade
advancing from the lawn,
blade on trembling blade.

Paris

The beds are so close
in this small hotel
by the Gare de Nord
you'd think we were married.
In the humid darkness
it feels as if we sleep on leaves.

Rain, falling like gravel,
wakes me in the middle of the night.
He breathes close by.
I think how wild animals
keep their distance,
but what they catch, they eat.

Slow Sunday

Is there pain among the pines
when an owl drops in flight
a ball of bone and fur?
Is it given up bitter as

wormwood, the way we give up
resentment of what love might
have made? All afternoon I
sit in the bar reading some

new poet and drinking brandy.
It's a slow Sunday. Outside
a storm is piling up winter.
Finally, the new lover of my lover

speaks to me. Half drunk,
I say with my eyes, "I want
you both." But he is too shy.
Is there pain in the night

when my sister's cats pass
the labor of their cares?
Does it leave like the years
squeezed from memory,

delicate with orange and spice,
secret as the moon moves?
Does it hurt till we pass
empty like a ball of light?

Low Clouds

It's rained for three days.
Now a mass of low clouds rolls by —
it is as if the earth were pulled

through a tunnel of flesh or wool.
I read your last letter again.
Slowly the winds are diminished.

The twin revolts of spirit and sky,
thoughts of revenge and thunder,
dissipate. The worst is done.

I feel relief mixed with wonder,
like when something made of glass
drops but does not break.

Winter Solstice

With cadence from the gathered hours,
a foil of water drips in intermittent
skip against the window pane.
Outside this dim lit winter room
the tan and spiny trees are slick
with moisture from an afternoon of rain.
Behind the trees, a row of buildings,
stone and gray, descends across the avenue.
Their line of wet-black roofs divides the spalled
facades from winter sky wrung pale with clouds.

There is a plague of shadows here.
Plants and cuttings press against
the glass to find the short December light.
Like dust the shadows fade on corduroy
that folds around the couch and chair.
Shadows smoke the corners and the sills.
There is a shadow cast around his form
that darkens all he wears or holds,
there is a darkness round his eyes
that shadows all his eyes behold.
It lingers on his spotted hands even when
a flame attempts to gild the liqueur in his glass.

There are shadows from December days
that follow me about this room.
I move from guest to guest and hope
I can avoid the shadow of his glance.
Must I remember once I knew him in the sun,
ablaze with our desire, and then
he turned obscure and walked away.

The Drive From Work

I could be like Cratylus and just point
With my finger at the damp light
Of afternoon that falls to the west.
See, thin clouds bleed twilight

Across a watercolor atmosphere.
From Harlem the road rises to a ledge,
Then the slow fall down to distance.
Up there you can see a wide wedge

Of traffic below the flannel sky.
Outlined by electric red and white,
The cars extend perspective to a dot,
Just like a fallen spear of light.

I can't help but think of you falling too,
Then caught stiff by that necklace
Of rope, which snapped your neck —
You fell so suddenly from our embrace,

You fell so far, Jerry, secret and alone,
To stall beneath the pale moon
That watches dumb as philosophic stone
The files of winter traffic going home.

The Scar on the Hand of the Porno Star

Admitting I see it, is admitting I see the rest;
but the stopping-dead-in-your-tracks beauty,
the prodigious stance with tool for trade,
the sharp blue eyes with their ring of sky
and core of slate, the oiled blond skin,
filling a perfect proportion of limbs,
that is not what I see again.
My eyes can't leave the faint red line
of a scar that runs down your thumb.
I got a scar like that too when as a boy
I worked the factory and opened my flesh
along with a shipping carton because I
resented the early hours, the lost freedom,
the drudgery of working in an endless hall
of dust and twisted filaments of light.
So, where comes yours, a fight, the farm,
the carelessness of one who just recently
discovered the price of beauty, fair-trade,
on the left hand too, working for a living.

Summer Solstice

The sun slips behind west buildings.
Pink and purple clouds hang
above a black silhouette of walls.
We had lunch under an umbrella,
talked about art—even though we give
our word, the world changes —
soft panels of light partition the hours.

Now the streetlights go on —
polka dots against blocks of blue.
A hum of night engines rubs against dust
as long limbs of the day relax into shadows.
The window is open and the radio on.
I could be holding him—dancing —
feeling my way in the dark.

From Dust to Dust

I take my spade and turn over the ground
by the roses. It cuts clean, this spear
heart, in the dry soil, clean into the gray
flesh of the earth, gray like boiled meat,

gray like clouds of incense ash,
or pickled bodies of the dead. So this is
the mixture roses use to make their blood.

I gave mother a rose that Sunday we drove
for steaks. We passed the cemetery where
father stays and I could not help notice
how her gaze lingered on the pastures

of stone, how she tried to say something
about a city of ash, and I seeing her
go cold, knew her mind had hold of earth,

the gray dust of our end. I knew my gift
of a rose was a gift for the underworld,
the gift of fire against the claims of dust,
a touch and go attempt, like the very way

weeks later in a bar, that boy with skin
smooth as a rose played touch and go
with my desire, all night, till after many

vodkas I decided to ask him if he dances.
"Not very good, no!" he said.
I shut my eyes against the lights and din
and fall into his gray and separate dust.

The Artist Held in Memory

Before a landscape in a gilded frame,
I feed on silence and white walls.
What is memory, except some hope
In face of the intractable world?

A voice tells me to forget my body.
Let a decade of desire fall to the floor
Like the crumbling folds of a silk robe.
Our flesh will only inherit loneliness.

The wounded wait a cure—the dead
Wait to rise. When sunlight breaks
Through the leaves with a shine
Of glycerine, I wait to see him again.

Even at night, when I kissed his lips,
The odor of balsam lingered in his hair.
It comes here now, among the whispers
And a hum of manufactured air.

A Descent to Darkness on Extended Wings

For Jerry Jaselski

Folds of light fall from the clouds
like a curtain drawn over the lake.
Come closer, can you place the voice?
Words are what the spirit wants for wings.

To see the bow of earth, the curve
of shore with its stubble of trees,
is to see past the skin of things.
In more ways than one we remember.

Broken by clouds, the light rains down,
then hides, to go, and come again
like the blue-gray pleading of our bodies.
A lifetime passes in a moment, a moment

informs a lifetime—the curtain of age
falls across our days the way a melanoma
of storms combs the shore of Michigan,
darkening the horizon—there are times

when we can only sing our pain to the sky,
no different from anyone else who has felt
how bodies come and go, leaving a remnant
to be read, as I read in clouds, a remnant

of empires or the dust of lost settlements.
Believe me, he was radiant with life too,
sitting by the window, his left hand
draped over his knee like a cloth of light.

All Saints Day

From my high window an expanse of streets
goes on forever, distance seems a sacred measure —
who can throw a bridge across the impossible
span of a lifetime, unwind the strings of solitude?

Father is dust, mother dust, Jerry dust too,
all scattered to the winds of memory,
scattered so only words can assemble
what they were, only words remember.

Take their names, the signature of each life,
write it out, cross your finger, make a wish.
Below, trains snake their way from the city,
long hauled silver, rolling into smoke.

Remembering Aschenbach

A long vein
runs the length
of that tan boy's leg.

I see it swell sea green
when he stands like a crane
to put on his gym shoe;

it pulses with blood —
salt like the sea
and foam too —
splashed across his hips.

Winter Fire

The fire falls like living glass
And shakes itself to flame again.
Beneath the grid fall orange and ash
From cords of pine and kindling cane.

The fire falls to flame anew,
And drops a weight of glowing stones —
Just like my old desire for you —
Still burning on this grid of bones.

Jim's Bright Eyes

For James M. Roy

The world was gray and dull and plain,
A time of neither love nor hate.
Then I saw you and we talked again.
How nice to join our words of late.

I look into your eyes and then away,
Then back upon their glittering bands.
Now neither wants to break the play,
Nor snap the bubble in our hands.

Eyes are the windows to the soul.
Your glance is like a gem that brings
The view of green and sunny meadows
And feathers fallen from some wings.

Resurrection

It is a long way coming to this place. Years
are spent trying to match a word with desires,
then beholding the great desire behind them all.

One thing leads to another, they say in analysis.
Can you feel it, the affair of the world surging
behind your back, metaphors glued to your hair

like tar, similes sticking to your honey finger?
It is a hard way for many, struggling out of their
parents' dream, saying what they know

in their own language of stones or candles.
What is love, but one turning away and the other
holding on? This is why some are ground sharp,

while others stay dull, biting their tongue.
We need time to tell of going out and coming back.
Visions run ahead, while words limp behind.

When we get there, the tomb is empty.
The ceremony of hearts falls away like a veil.
Spell this victory if you know how.

At the Beach

Two lovers slosh out of the water,
dragging behind them the ropes of time.

Sand sticks to their feet—rocks and shells
milled down to grains of annoyance.

"What else in the world is as beautiful
as we two?" they ask with an embrace.

One after another the waves follow,
breaking themselves into foam.

The Rare Music of a Russian Icon

For David Wilcox

"It is the season of shaking loose.
Trees, still green, have in their leaves
a whisper of retreat. It is a season of shrinking —
September—long blue shadows on the wall.

"Sometimes it is a pinprick, sometimes a sword,
the way memories of loss come back —
and music makes it bleed so much the more.
Accused of being barren, forced to take the veil,
I play in musty rooms with icons of the saints.

"What is it that pulls me back to these melodies —
A summer house, a stockade fence, the road,
a dry time before the shroud of snow?
I did not want my love to end with treachery.

"We grow to awareness, as the great fir tree
grows into space above the cloister, spreading
here and there, filling the air around its home
with needles—this is how I filled my space—
that is all—that is all our grave demands.

"Abandonment is the only music:
father, friends, husband, a world of faces

darken under soot and smoke and wax.
How years of yearning spread a veil of ash.

"In dreams I realize I set my life so that
this theme will play itself again and again.
Victim, sacrifice, the sea abandoning its shells,
the sky its birds, the trees their leaves —
all players toss their music to the wind.

"My loss, your loss, those are the only dreams
we clutch at midnight with the pillowslips.
In sleep I say his name, in life I note it well,
and balance both upon the figure of a cross.

"The melody moves, measure by measure,
into the sorrow we come to love.
It holds the pulse and pause of autumn's age,
and every now and then, a sullen youth
who reads the notes gets up to turn the page."

To All the Heterosexuals Whose Lives Are Heavy as Stone

I look about and see their monuments
outlined in bright, blue sunshine.
They have taken so much from us,
we are free in spite of ourselves.

Garlands made of stone flowers
stay frozen forever in their lazy
drape between the colonnades.
Where are the signatures of ghosts?

Such gravity among the dead —
mortgage, tuition, the silence
between them thick as moss,
time's cold dehydration.

And we, who are left to our own
devices, sun and shadow dividing
our cleft names on the forum,
we have learned how easy it is

to survive, how lightweight
our testimony, like the careless burden
of birds who say with antics above
the tombs, "See, we are different."

Could the Heart At Ease Still Love,
Or Is that Ease Being in Love?

I look carefully at the sunlit window.
There is something written on the glass,
and something more behind the glass.

I see the same light when I look in his eyes,
searching for the right word, the word
that mirrors what is gone. Looking for words

is like looking for water—there on the tip of
my tongue, the letter, the drop, the thirst,
a flurry of angels guarding the alphabet.

I wonder about the presence that resides
behind words. Is it like the presence of a man
besides his body? How does it happen? Here.

Gone. Memory. Letters trying to drink.
Words thirsty to be said. A scripture of eyes.
Go easy now or the book runs over, so long dry.

Perhaps he is the one to rinse away my rust.
And what of the rest? There are arid pages
where death declares, *Do not disturb my dust.*

Moses Is Told He Cannot Cross Over

I bring Christopher to help George set up his computer. George is old now and in a wheelchair. I sit on the overstuffed sofa and listen as Christopher explains all the steps of the program. George learns easily when the teacher is handsome. I lean back and listen to the sound of Christopher's voice. I have grown used to it, and follow it up and down in my mind, relishing how a man's voice is as much a sign of his being as his fingerprints. It is late June and the day is warm and humid. Insistent sunlight pries its way through the blinds to the floor. The overhead fan hums away. I count myself lucky to be here with Christopher. I look at the clutter of boxes that litter George's apartment. Copies of old newspapers yellow in the corner. Flat on the desk is a gray photo of George when he was eighteen. How dark his hair was then. A carton of milk warms on the table. A can of tomato juice, wedged open, leaks a ring on the counter top. I see some dirty clothes rolled up on the floor of the next room. Still, with patience, Christopher explains the function of this key and that. George is going to write his life story once the computer is fixed. It is a long story, he says, filled with war and regret. Christopher and I only visit for a while, but it is one of those moments where three men hold themselves up by voices in an atmosphere that is reverent and complete. Even the soda cans on the windowsill glow not from metal but from grace. I think maybe the boxes piled high could be stones in the wall of the Old Temple. Christopher's voice rises like the sweet smoke of an offering. Lord, what a mess, and what a mess love forgives.

Postcard

In the gray light of early morning,
flags of fog wave up from the black river.
I am away from home, studying
the steam from my teacup,

and watching ghosts lift their
ethereal bodies from graves of water.
Who comes here? Kant, Hegel,
Wittgenstein, all speaking at once.

What vessel holds so many spirits
but language: see, from
this page, like a fog, desire rises,
and is sent to another place.

Read me as I write my heart, read
across the stars the fog that is
our wonder, our reaching, our wish.
Between black and white we wait.

The sun moves up behind a row of trees,
a fish jumps, and splashes back
into the obsidian mirror of the river.
The diamond edge of light polishes letters.

This is how it is alone and writing.
Voices, down by the dock, assemble
parts of the day, a boat sails out.
Read how the waters tremble.

Leaving Greenwood

The vats of night pour out their indigo.
Some dots of light from cars are all I see.
Forgetfulness is mixed with vertigo.
I could be held in space or lost at sea.

The one whom I desired, the many who lied,
What matter they beneath the open sky?
I roll right past the pledge that lived and died,
And pistons push the memory farther by.

No mind can number all the men whose names
Have rattled through the show of bars and streets,
Or all the kings and queens and royal games
That send the soldiers out to stomp their cleats.

White columns hold up balconies of ferns,
And garlands tie the air with ribbons of spice.
Indifferent to the poverty that burns,
The fatted guests enjoy champagne on ice.

Just line them up, the golden-haired, the lame,
The ones I loved: a beautiful disdain
Allows them all to pass, yet prize their name.
No matter what, must poets go insane?

I settle back, the world will carry me.
In time our silent, spacious graves approach
With nameless grace, and possibility.
The engine fires on and hauls the coach.

It happens now I make my trip at night,
And read the words God married to a cross.
Above the woods the winter stars look bright—
Love follows love and loss releases loss.

Repondez, S'il Vous Plait

For Rodney Lee Krafka

Snow falls into night. Perturbed by desire,
I wonder why my middleage does not decide
for spirit instead of flesh? We were never both students
from the broken fields of Nebraska, yet, I see him
in my mind's eye gliding through the water of his high
school pool, reaching and reaching, even across to Paris,
and then reaching up from the fields at midnight where
the stars are white dots above a script of battling trees.

A gray river runs under the bridges of our city.
Above the river the moon lingers.
I know he and Michael broke open the windows
of laughter once; and later, when Susan looked
a long time into his eyes, he did not go with her
to the party, but thought instead, I prefer my books.
What are we all running from, I ask? "Father,
take back these keys, they do not open what I want."

For years nothing has worked right in my heart.
One gear was too big, another too small.
Now these words wind up a page the way snow
fills up the street. We are old enough to love.
It would be good to ride the heat of his legs.

There are lines on our chart that say it is best.
Sitting in a crowd I hear his voice in my mind
as talk in the room dulls to a cushion of smoke.

Clocks melt, calenders drown, his profile is holy
in the world as the diminimus days advance.
All year long my hands have held a body of dust.
In the capitol there are rooms of marble and mirrors.
In the featureless ocean sharks circle and feed.
What means our small gentleness here
to the great schemes of power and blood?
It is not necessary to go farther—I open my hands.

How may it end, I wonder? It is a snowy afternoon.
Ribbons caught in a tree branch slap with the wind.
The car door opens and he throws in his backpack.
Our eyes meet, then turn away. My life is in pills,
his is in words—father of the sky, father of the books,
your law of the world holds sway over such gestures.
The car door slams shut. He drives away—
or, there may be music and we dance.

Conundrum

The last time I saw Earl, he was shopping at the Everthing-For-A-Dollar-Store. His skin was the color of iodine, and he stood by the knickknacks, holding a plastic bowl. I watched him as he looked at it, as if in a trance, resting the bowl in his palm, his fingers relishing the shape and texture. The stuff of his heart was glued to it. He then picked up a glass and studied the light that played off the rim. He held it so hard, it could have cut him. I imagine that is the hard way he held his wife, too, and she cut him. Thus, we are made for the world. Just touch it. There is your proof. Here are no airy spirits in search of philosophy. Here is a man adhering to flesh, and the matter and glory of this world. His knuckles are white from clenching so long, yet he is unable to hold even the cold water of winter. There are no art colonies here, with bay windows opening to the sea, or country houses with studios, and afternoon tea with silver, brocade and roses everywhere. This is not the place where art moves forward into death, and we contemplate it like the dark side of the moon. We are not making a future God by our discipline and a plethora of gadgets. Here are parking lots and high-tension wires, here are diesel exhaust and whining engines, here are plate-glass windows and cash flow, cancer and chemotherapy, touching, clinging, wishing. Here, the body simply calls to us as if from the depths of a well. Even when we are forced to let it go, we think the troubled world is good. I bet on the windswept steppes of Russia, where burlap doubles for skin, morose peasants plead with their bones to hold them up, too. They say there are three things that come as a surprise: a silver coin found in the street, the sting of a scorpion, and the Kingdom of God. Right now, I allow the hands of recognition to wring what is sour from my words and hope for a surprise. In a northern forest of fir and pine, a stag scours his antlers on a branch. The crust of snow cracks beneath his hooves. We hold the baubles of life in our hands, and do not want to let go, our baby fingers pressed around a digit of stars. There is a white whistle in the air as the arrow sings to his heart.

Fire at the Old Factory

The factory where my father used to work,
  the old Cuneo Press,
    burnt down.

It closed some time after he died,
  then sat idle for years,
    and later was used to store old tires.

When the piles of tires caught fire,
  after holding themselves in abandonment
    so long, the building burned for a week.

The fire department had to pump water from the river
  on the smoldering ruins—a deep glow of hot rubber
    rumbled like indigestion in the old boilers.

As I ride by now, I get a glimpse of burnt tires,
  twisted like charcoal pyramids,
    piled on the assembly floor.

I see the broken windows and bindery walls
  where thousands of men worked,
    just like you.

Time clocks, black lunchboxes with sandwiches
  wrapped in the frost of waxed paper,
    smells of ink, sweat, beer—they all return.

On the corner you would catch the streetcar
  down Archer to come home,
    eat boiled sausage on a white plate,

hold your head in your hands,
  while your elbows
    dampen the dark wood of our table.

You know, father,
 for a long time I've been smoldering
  with your memory,

the absence you manufactured
 has collected like old rubber
  to fuel the flames over these long years.

Why, the other day,
 as I was tying my shoes,
  I looked up and thought I saw you

seated at the table,
 I wanted to ask
  if you found a wisdom I overlooked,

for both of us are men now,
 and I've lived in the world
  working, making up for my loss.

"So father," I say to myself,
 "What think you of my love,
  my learning, my livelihood?

Would you like a drink,
 is there water sweet enough
  to dull the fire of our long farewell?"

Old Movies

Old movies remind me
of the antique world
my father left by dying.
He saw slow, black cars
jerk over cobbled streets,
bottles of milk
resting on shiny oilcloth,
iceboxes made of wood.

Father was an iceman.
He hauled his frozen bulk
from wife to widow.
A leather shield on his back
was always damp with ice melt.
After he died, we'd play
in the basement
with the iron tongs he used.

I imagine those tongs today
pointed as the ones the devil has
to drag scoffing souls off to hell,
pointed as the glycerin needle
the doctor slid into his heart.
But it was too late, no medicine
could melt the hold ice had on him.

He left us with nothing much,
just small change mother used
to bundle us off every Saturday
to the movies, where, for a quarter,
we watched cold heroes
flicker with electric fire.

Epithalamium

It always hurts,
the lodestone in our thighs,
Sometimes we laugh to see
where wrestling got us

but it hurts —
not a wound, nor blood, but
being lost on a lost continent —
please find us in the flames.

Still Life With Sunrise

At dawn, flocks of gulls renounce the lake
and fly off west to feed—their cries,
like the cries of babies, fade to silhouettes
of wings that flap from water up to the air.

Something is happening above the trees—
still at attention, but tinged with trembling.
They are cautious of the light September brings.

I read the trembling written in the air
against the words of childhood lost like birds.
Where is duty, where is fear, a sacred routine
of water birds assures the dawn unwinds.

My mother, in the garden of memory, goes out
in the morning too, with a basket for flowers.
Her skirt collects the dew like pearls.

I watch the beauty of her naked blade.
Zinnias, cut off like straws, give up their
platforms of color to grace a table by the window.
A light through gauze will play on their perfume.

If angels wrapped with robes of silk come close,
they surely bend amazed to see our ways.
The girl who spreads her legs like wings, the boy

who rides the midnight of the peacock's eye,
the man who stays bewildered in the waste of seeds,
these are what the angels see, then pause like gulls,
to curl away in whirlpools of brittle leaves.

New Wine, Old Wine

I propose a wedding feast of sand and nails.
What slips through your fingers, what draws blood?
All they want is for us to be silent, then die,
and pull the silence, like earth, around us.

But I can't—every stone is a text, every text
a shield against the black arrows of time.
And when there comes a time where words cannot
work, gestures pays homage to the imagination.

Do you remember, as a child, how big the world
of just your street seemed, how long the days?
Older now, it all seems so small, that bedroom,
that house, that neighborhood on the edge

of oblivion. I traveled to India once,
the outpost of dreams, and returned to see dry
leaves falling, to see stones, white in the sun,
to read them as I read a destiny in my palm.

Now I imagine the small world, round in the sky.
Is not all creation present to the mind of God?
These leaves, falling in their own good time,
is simply the way the stage of our days is set.

So why am I desperate, kicking my feet
through this pile of discard, are they not
just notes falling from the trees, scripts
from the stars, love letters sent and lost?

And this display of complicated gestures,
so many gloves, so many letters scattered
across the desk of the street, it's simply rubbish—
help me, help me pick them up, read their address.

Maybe I can glue them all back on their stems,
put the waste of the world back in place,
repair the trees—but there are so many, whole
arms full, and the stars, so many more too.

The holy freedom of the heart opens to words,
I don't have to do it over. What is done is gone.
Even though a hollow in the bone, milked by time,
will never close, it is all right, starting now

I may exhaust the sentiments inherent in sand.
Drop by drop is one way to reduce the days.
Now the dry books begin to smell of old leaves,
and his skin reads like parchment to my touch.

THREE POEMS FOR KABBALAH

1. Playing Ball With Keagan

A boy, about eleven, anxious to escape the eye
of his dour mother, dives into the swimming pool
after a yellow ball. His splash breaks the honeycomb
of light that reflects off the surface of the water.

I decide to jump in and swim as well.
Throw me the ball, I say to the boy,
and all too willing to make a friend, he throws it.
We begin to play a game of toss and catch.

How long can we keep the ball up, without dropping?
39, 40, 41, we jump and fall, cushioned by water.
Soon we wear the cellophane and silver jewelry
of the bather's dance, to lose it all, and gain

the more, as we splash back to the sound of soft glass
breaking into sheets of light. Will we make 613?
Will we keep the commandments of light and water?
The talisman is tossed higher with hope.

Look, I have now forgotten what I am. Later, I will
see how the flame of love lives in water, and that
as the scroll of years unrolls, we wait to clothe
ourselves in it, in the light that is above the water,

but now I only wonder how long we may play this.
And the boy, as old as I was when my father died,
what becomes of him, how glad he is to please,
how blushed with my approval when he hears me say,

Nice save, how blessed we two are just now playing.
So it goes, back and forth, until he has to leave
for lunch, and I resume my waiting in the sun.
By words worlds are sustained, worlds are destroyed.

Such playfulness must be the point of daily prayer,
the sorcery of the sabbath; thus we cannot write
desire on the water, no leaven here, just the spirit
hovering above our bodies, bright as mirrors.

If only I could grab from air all the words I need.
How impossible it seems, day after day,
tossed between the sun and moon like a rubber ball,
then waking up tomorrow, not a muscle sore.

2. The Moan of the Ram's Horn

The night before my mother died
I combed her gray hair and rubbed
her forehead with lotion. Now I watch
the old newsreels about the end of the war.

A woman like my mother sits on a Paris bench.
She smiles and wears a flowered print dress,
like the ones I remember my mother washing
and hanging out to dry in the back yard.

From the museum they show the yellow stars
that say *Jude* and one small shoe from
a child that went up in smoke.
My mother never saw the stars above Paris.

I came into the world after the camps
were open, their aroma of suffering hissing
into memory like the rush of roasted coffee
when a silver nail opens the vacuum of a can.

The night before my mother died I combed her hair.
I saw in her eyes an opening into questions,
a pasture of longing beyond her body.
The newsreels flicker with their scratchy songs.

Have you seen a dry leaf swept up
by a turmoil of wind and blown around
with the wild unrolling of time?
So the ways of the world release us,

and we pass into the emptiness that makes
possible the music of a chime, the moan
of the ram's horn, so the song of angels fills
the emptiness of God as the blood reaches

for something more; a ruby, a fire, a rose.
You won't need that other shoe, child.
You won't need that hair or that yellow star.
You won't need that flowery dress.

Tomorrow we will anoint her eyes.
The grass is soft, the sky is wide open.

3. Tsimtsum

After a swirl of starlings, night settles in.
To that darkness I drive alone, surrendering
my desire with the ebb and flow of words.

I collect blue glass for my room, so I collect
the blue glass of night, just as the sky's
limbs gather the cobalt glow of a star's seed.

Here I roll by, caught up in a river of traffic,
but there is still time to see the old, lame man
in his wheelchair stopped on the sidewalk.

How long does it take to realize a prophet
is crippled and spends his days looking into
the heart of the world, where he sees

not an emptiness silk traders cameled across
the desert, but simply the apple of mystery?
There he see the mystery mistaken for emptiness.

O holy days of songs and speed, magic and
memory at our fingertips—they used to teach
after Auschwitz there could be no more poems,

but here we are, American survivors of *Mutterland
und Vaterland*, wrapped in our silver wheelchairs,
and the words are still mouthed, hanks of hair, ash,

drums for our lovers gone to bone, while the moon
rises over rails of traffic, over the lacquered box
of hell, where our fearless angels still prevail.

The Rampart Cavalcades

For Kevin Stein

Knobs of colored lights and chrome,
Pendant baskets spilling over with flowers,
A wall of TVs, recombinant images:
None of it works. I still think about him.
Why did I come to a bar crowded with men
Who offer their ice to pillars of salt?

Smoke another cigarette.
That click, scratch, flame from a Zippo
Is a complete ritual. Damn,
Wednesday I go for my blood test.
Have another drink. Right now,
I am not above stealing what I want.

Today, all the way up the brick wall,
Hands of ivy begged alms from the sun.
On this green screen I saw his face.
Our defeated desire is begging like ivy.
How else will freedom happen except
The days of the world bring it about?

Across the city marriage plans are made.
Ropes are let out. Knots tied. Ribbons cut.
I am willing to take from him the way
Another took from me. What will we do?
I hear the glass music of blessings break.
Where's mine? The nomads move on.

Searchlights play metronome on the sky.
The stars are washed away by a bright haze
From the city. For some reason, God gave
The boy at the table next to me a crippled body.
Still, it is good they found each other —
The world lives another day.

A new generation is knocking on the gate.
I look up from my coffee, and see them,
Full of life, their hair strung with light.
They give their bodies to one another
Carelessly. So, why am I still sitting here?
Because I was paralyzed by a kiss.

Now is the *rush hour of the gods.*
Buddha chants to bass guitars.
Boys whiten their hair, they want to look old.
Lead us by our rings to oblivion, they pray.
So, the cry goes out, *rave, rave,
Rave against the dying of the night.*

Techno-trash children lounge in doorways
And stare up at me like prisoners for sacrifice.
I am on my way to meet him, wondering
If the right words will fall in my lap.
They tell me a new community is being born.
Look, neither their clothes nor their ideas fit.

The ghost of Heidegger rides with the ad
On the side of the bus: *be once, be always,
Just be.* Madison Avenue's plea for
Authenticity. Clever, by saying it you
Deny it. Church bells clamor—think of
The man who digs a grave for his child.

In a dream we are swept up from the street
By soldiers and forced to wear striped suits.
An old woman behind a curtain hands me
A coat. I refuse it, and hide my papers.
We are separated. I find him. We go underground.
He is atop me. His key unlocks my mouth.

From a gray, malodorous drop to a dusty box,
That is the course of man's life under the sun.
Yet I am still here arguing with my body,

Arguing with my age—love tastes good,
But the memory of love gone is wormwood.
Doctor, how many specimens need you collect?

One did not believe and was trampled at the gate.
Another was excluded for muttering names
Over wounds, yet I write his name,
And say it in the street, hoping he hears
To offer me the light of his face and hands.
Say it slowly, add the letters, the sum is, *yes.*

Time's brass pendulum cuts off ark after ark of air.
In this world some fruit falls before it is ripe.
Pages drop in the river of confusion that flows
Past my door. Where is the current going?
They say, in the world to come, this assembles
To a city with jeweled walls and gardens.

Silver trains transcribe the bridge,
Black and white reflections write ripples
On the river, flags stretch and then relax.
Light flows down the long canyon
Of streets from a window in the clouds.
His voice calls open what sleeps in me.

Day after day I read the wrinkled mail.
So many desperate scribes pecking away
Like chickens at the scattered corn of words.
A continent of blank pages waits for a rain
Of letters to end the drought, to write on them:
This is the name of what you love.

Yet is not today about being tender
And sewing up wounds with the glory of hands,
Is it not about trusting one another in the dark,
Is it not nights and days, is it not offering
Our clotted words, is it not the light
Of a companion shining in the darkness?

Stones only know the weight that keeps
Them down. For them, love and wisdom
Are the same silence. Joy is not to move,
And death itself is a kind of motion.
Do we wound stones when we lift them up?
Wound some men and words pour out.

What cannot change in me is made like stone.
My love is my weight. I have been warned.
It is like warning a pillar. Read these
Inscriptions. They rest on the bedrock
Of childhood: father, mother, book.
Here is slate, here is chalk, here!

Born nervous into a morning of clouds,
I listen for the gallop of far-off horses.
Could I take a part from the men I love
And put them together to make the puzzle
Of desire complete? What is missing?
Father, his kiss is such tenderness.

He dislodged something loose in me, and now
It is falling, falling the way a stone falls
To the floor of a white canyon, falling
The way a dancer who leaps falls.
We wait and listen, the feather pauses,
and when it hits, silence explodes.

They wandered in the desert for forty years.
There were no gems or gold to bring home,
Only dust from the well of words. Take it.
Make a tent. Make an alabaster dome.
Make a cushion in your heart, pillow my fall.
This is all the wealth I have to share.

On the eve of the ninth of Ab, these are
Forbidden: the joy of study, scented oils,
And the pleasures of love—so it is written.
Carry my desire out of the city in a coffin.

In a room filled with light from high windows
A man touches our prayers to a piano.

Before the poet there is the dream hunter.
The sky is everywhere and for the taking.
I watch him sleep. His pulse follows the dream.
The black hood of the falcon is removed.
There is a flutter of wings like breath.
He rips raw vowels from the bone of love.

Across the harbor white boats point to the wind.
A black lace of rigging scratches the sky
And deltas downward to a forest of masts.
Is it not likely the dead will rise?
If you look at letters long enough, shapes
Appear: sails, chariots, who knows what?

Such is the pardon my letters buy.
Do not be afraid, I write as if poems were
A proposal, when they are simply sign
After sign, rose after rose, an apostrophe
In place of pain. Maybe it works!
Draw the shade. Light the lamp. Write.

Crisscrossed Names

It is winter and the crows caw
their song of woe to the damp, gray air.
I try to read the trees' black letters.
I do not know the name they write.

What is the missing word?
I mourn the death of something,
but walking here in day's darkness,
I can't say rightly what it is.

A part of me, perhaps the way I am
tied to events, has not held up well.
I leak. Drop by drop my desire
to hold on to names runs out.

Instead, I hear a shuffle of papers,
see the eventual stamp of loss,
and dull glycerin clogging our veins.
Down and across are of a piece.

Would any answer made from words
fill the space time leaves open?
Hardly, air into air is more air.
Only children see faces in the clouds.

Just half the alphabet has roots.
The other half is proof, by reading
out loud, my wandering heart
must make a home in wandering.

Homework

A man works all day. He doesn't worry about the emotional life of animals. He wants to come home to a plate of ribs and a cold beer. He wants to sit still and stare at his plate. He wants to remember one who did not love him, and why. A man works all day and comes home and wonders if he will have enough money for Saturday, or enough money to buy a book or some more beer. A man works all day in the city and wonders why the people down the block only painted two numbers on their gate and left the other to be written in pencil. A man wonders why the legs of a boy are soft, but when you touch them, boys look out at the sky with blank eyes. Boys do not know themselves as beautiful and cannot imagine how their soft legs can be as food for a man who works all day in the city and is hungry to touch something he has lost and must find groping in the dark like a blind man. A man works all day and comes home to a plate of ribs and a beer and wonders where his childhood has gone. He looks at his hands. He looks at his legs. Were they once soft? He remembers when he was twelve and how his friend Ronald would show him how to find hidden places while riding their bikes. He remembers going to Ronald's house once and seeing him naked in the tub. He tried to be a boy then, too, and stare into space, but he knew in his heart what he wanted. It was too late to ever be a boy again. A man comes home from work tired and thinks about the rich man in his high house, the chandeliers, the woman in furs, the goblets of champagne and bowls of oysters. He looks at his hands and looks at his feet. He sees the broken glass of his life in pieces on the floor. He sweeps them up and dumps them in the trash. A man comes home from work tired and turns on the light by the tan armchair. He picks up his book and reads how we should be shipwrecked in faith. He thinks of the sunshine of Sicily and the boys of Taormina, tan and naked among the rocks. Their legs and arms and stomach are soft to touch. He thinks of crusty bread and amphoras of golden olive oil. A man comes home from work and shuts his eyes. He dreams. He sleeps. The night bleeds into tomorrow. A man gets up and goes to work.

Poor Apology

It is a late autumn afternoon.
I can almost see the sun move,
orange and weighted with our hours.
For a moment light is reflected
through the Palladian window,
spilling bright bands of gold
across the parquet floor.
"Look here," it seems to say,
"Flesh is heir to a promise."

I know he is dying. Cancer.
But like a fool, I say, "Hi,
how ya doin' ?" We talk anyway,
careful to use metaphor.
After a few words, some sherry,
the light is gone lower,
sinking, repressed as rage
beneath a civil afternoon.
Blue shadows dust my shoes.

He showed me his spiral,
screwed notebook once.
It held pencil-thick jottings,
words of lead and radium.
I pretend I cannot read his hand.
To myself I say, "Can any of this

help: these seasonal moods,
this supposed Chinese art
of imitating emptiness?"

Afterwards, driving home
down the slow slope of the hill,
I plan to make apology.
The air is rustic with perfume.
A pallid sun trips light
along a row of picket trees.
Dry leaves run after the car,
bark their wild colors
like a pack of hounds.

Overnight by English Bay

Eagle, raven, bear holding man,
Thunderbird—totem poles erect
among the cedars and fog.
Careful not to wake him
I write home that
the azaleas are aflame,
their petals fall
like drops of candle wax.
There are so many gardens here
I fear the flowers will make me blind.

I watch his moods,
the scent of smoke and cedar.
We grow close —
stop —
changing moods
like light across the slopes,
or moving with the tide
lapping at the shore of English Bay,
the tide that alternates
across the weed-wet rocks
and pools of lingering.

He tells me
every man's secret
is a shadow on his heart.
I hope the darkness falls
to constant light.
I hope his heart falls to light
much like the dawn
so soft upon his length.
It holds the little sounds of sleep
and folds in careless shades
across his scattered clothes.

Dim Conjunctions

"Gently," he whispers to himself
as he confides to the secret object
of his desire, gently, like a fog
that for days has kept the world
to the shape of this dim locality.

Gently, in the darkness, the light
from lamps, neon signs, yellow shafts
from windows and doors, the brown
and tans of November lit with electric,
all mingle in the air. As substance

the light damps the atmosphere,
giving to shadows the partial solidity
they would have in the land of death,
giving to the globes of bright color
the mystery they have as clots of life.

Gently the world absorbs the sounds
of traffic, the hesitant hiss of wind
as it slides across leather leaves,
as the dim conjunctions of buildings
and clouds are like watercolors run.

Gently the weight of work accomplished
subsides with the length of breaths,
and sitting there, by a window open
to the colors of night captured in each
small drop of mist descending to moss,

he imagines his need for being touched
to be like that of moist air upon the night,
neither hard nor demanding, a simple gesture
like the ways of water, like the way
a hand laid on our shoulder calls us back.

Conversation

Since we never married,
I am allowed to remember
how I would come home late
and imagine you waiting.

I look up from the street
and see the window open.
In the yellow light our curtains
stumble with parallel desire.

Tonight I lie late in bed,
sleepy with the draw of years.
The window is half open.
A pleasant breeze carries in

chatter from chestnut avenues,
and the tender rustle of leaves.
They are talking to me
the way I would talk to you.

Hands

"November's green begins to grain the grass.
The edge of growth spills out like colors
on a blotting cloth. A day or two and brown
bush buds will break. It is spring on the pampas.
With the architects and matrons we motor
from the city to Catamarca.
Pura señorita de Buenos Aries,
I sit, still in white and wait.
White dress with hand-sewn
lace, white shoes, white hat and gloves,
the second change my mother ordered worn today.
She and father talk of the hospital,
how the railroad pensioners will gain by it.
We are fortunate.
The company can use Indians as laborers.
We need not hire high-paid workers from the town.

"There is nothing here but field.
The men go off to tape and measure.
I walk alone around the cars,
worried by Indians squatting,
robbed like graven stone.
They have no shoes.
They wear no gloves.
Their eyes are dim like the room
where father smokes alone at night.
I hide my hands beneath my shawl.
Slowly, I slide off my gloves,
and let them see my hands naked.
I recall this now as the artist leaves.
I look through the curtains to the boulevard.
It is spring.
My husband wishes to commission my portrait.
He ordered me to dress in white.
The artist says he can do my head,
but charges more for hands."

Mozart and the Use of Light to Capture Loneliness

A writer is not a person with something to say,
but a person with something to write.

—*Roland Barthes*

A mortal weariness slumps down
like the colored trees of autumn, it happens
when we see through the ways of the world,
and know that whatever comes riding
on dappled horses or rolling with the wind
will be more of the same, more seasons
to spend the wild money of melodies and leaves.

Mozart, where does the music come from?
Is it sister to light, brother to words,
as simple as running; does it come down
like the Koran from the lips of an angel,
or the leaves of elms feathering the boulevard?
Does it bother you what I loved was like music,
and gums my memory as an indigestible lump?

Those early concertos seem too perfect.
Like fat Cupids painted in pastels
cavorting on a baroque ceiling in Prague,
they are immune to mortal particulars.
Yet it is on the hands of men and women
that your melodies live again, mortal fingers
pull the bows, tap the keys, counterpoint time.

Around the corner, a boy at the pizzeria
pushes a pizza into the oven's red mouth.
The last vagabond piece of the puzzle
that is today slides seamlessly into place.
Music and medallions fall from the sky.
He smiles, knowing it is work done right,
and dreams of love like lights under water.

Bughouse Square

For Barbara Korbel

The students of mist are out walking.
Fog, like the patina on old things,
seeps down from the morning sky.
A golden carpet of leaves covers
the park, while the damp branches
of balding oaks and elms
fork the clouds like mossy antlers.

Rain and autumn, a muffled wind
on a late October Saturday,
all help the leaves absorb the damp,
the way a memory of candle flames
absorbs the amber light of prayers.
Think about it, all those dry books
next door sleeping between boards,

all those mothers and fathers before,
sleeping beneath the folded earth,
covered with its blond shawl.
As willows and chrysanthemums
bend into moss, as stone stairs
shine with a red abandoning,
so much is just thrown away.

What scholar of puddles and pauses
could remember all the leaves and books,
stitch dim histories of bone and bruise,
or the worry and waste of counting?
Wet eye of the world I guess what you want,
letting the leaves fall even into night,
until we are held up by a redeeming light.

The Highway

For Ingrid Lesley

This morning the October moon
shines through my west window.
So bright and full, it casts
a shadow on the breakfast table.
Half a day later, as we drive south,
I see the same moon come up again,
cold eye of the night in the east.

There are six of us in the rusty van,
and a six-week-old baby.
When the baby cries, the older woman
holds it close to the moons of her breast.
"Oh, you have a lot to talk about,"
she says, as one who understands
this simple poetry of milk and tears.

I look out again at the harvest moon.
A cemetery of cornstalks flicks by.
Done crying for the dead, I welcome
the thin fellowship of reflected light.
Older now, I can tell you how it was —
my moonlight lover had such freckled
skin as to be food for my eyes.

Jeffrey Dahmer Stands Trial

I read in the newspaper about these
horrible crimes: rape, murder,
cannibalism, the cutting up of human
flesh and bones, and I remember

how frail we are, how delicate and
tender is the stuff of flesh, easily
slit, nothing to a saber saw.
When it snows now, I think it is

the salt of love falling from the sky,
or white bones, ground to dust
from the press of news, when it snows
I remember we were all delicate once.

Something flew out of him like a bird.
Was it conscience, a flock of crows
flapping, crying, caw, caw caw,
as feathers fanned the purple sky?

The banality of evil—sitting frozen
in a courtroom, silent, brooding.
Where is the necklace of skulls, the vermilion
robe, hair ashen like the floor of an oven?

The boy's body was the color of sea coral.
How Jeffrey ached to get his hands on it,
it was like singing when the knife cut
through the ham of his thigh like butter.

Centuries ago, a man wrote, "I recovered
this book from the river where it was thrown
by barbarians. I am poor, but by the grace
of God, I read, so I saved this book."

Later, a sheriff recovered hollow bones
from a field where they were thrown
by one who could not read the body —
a barbarian lover, all teeth and silicone.

"I gave them sleeping pills so it wouldn't
hurt, I thought if I kept drilling, I would
find it, that part of me. To my horror,
the darkness now is gum and sticks like tar."

Time remains a vast stretch of blood—
he has forever to reach what he cannot touch.
Salt frosts his hands like bleach.
"Oh hell, here is my poem of bones."

After Scotch and Soda

I think of elder men in polished rooms,
Alone with photographs in glass and gold,
Alone with china, crystal and heirlooms,
And realize how soon is growing old.
I think of younger men in wrinkled beds
Alone with heat and dreams and tossing sleep,
Alone with dancing shadows in their heads
And see how short a time in love we keep.
I think of men in middle age awhile
Who see behind the powers that youth abuse
And hope ahead the cure of wit and style,
I think of men alone and drunk who muse,

"I need no special powers of science or art,
To say I loved you and you broke my heart."

In Memory of All the Homosexuals
Who Were Cut in Half by Saws

Violence is the last resort of the exhausted sensibility.

—*Karl Shapiro*

I

Years ago, Sodomites were strung up by their legs,
spread eagle, arms tied down, then sawed in half.
Since that position allows blood to rush to the head,
it is assumed many were conscious and feeling pain
until the saw passed the navel, sometimes the heart.
I guess such torture is rooted in the erroneous belief
that all gays like it up the ass, so bring on the saws.

I know a young gay guy, he's cute, but doesn't read books.
He has no idea that homosexuals were punished by such
exquisite means years ago. He lives in a big American city
where he takes sex and freedom for granted,
the way we take for granted flying and abstract art.
He knows all Madonna's songs by heart.

II

There are always those who stand by and watch
when great horrors happen to the unfortunate.
Artists must do this to get the details right.
We have gapers' block on the expressways.
In a sixteenth-century German etching that shows
a Sodomite being sawed in half by the Inquisition,
the artist deftly outlines the layer of skin and fat
above the great muscles of the buttocks,
as a toothy saw rips through tissue and bone.
And then there are the two men who work the saw,
pulling and pushing, as if this flesh were a log
that had to be split into planks for furniture.
The screaming alone would tell them this was not wood,
but a human being, a man, not a side of beef,
then again, he was a fag, a homo, a queer,

butthole screwing Sodomite, and the nice thing
about civilization is that you can always find
people willing to do the dirty work for money.

Today, deep in a silo in North Dakota, two other men
have their fingers on scarlet buttons that will launch
thermonuclear fire on half the cities of the USSR.
One reads a comic book while the other works
a computer that rivals in complexity an insect brain.
He spends his leave in San Francisco drinking beers,
the other is from Texas, says he hates queers.

III

Roger is in the hospital, kept alive by tubes.
His friends are all whispers and worries.
On Fire Island, waves ignore the sick and lap ashore.
Near the deck of a beach house, a man
clothed in the cool whites of summer,
contemplates the simplicity of far away lights.
Two drinks sweat on a bamboo table.
A clove cigarette curls to ash in a shell.
He swirls his tonic with ice and takes a sip.

Above a mahogany desk, in the guest room,
an elegantly framed sixteenth-century etching
reminds us of the dark line of details
needed to maintain an illusion of reality.
The eye and the heart assemble from fragments
what they desire—like the trails protons leave
in a cloud chamber, there is evidence, but don't
bring it up, for now, only our red geraniums suffer.
Rich in blood they bleed into the black, absorbent night.

The Difference Between Then and Now Is That Then They Believed in Revolution

The dangers gather as the treasures rise.

—*Samuel Johnson*

A blind man stands in front of the Pittsfield
 Building and shakes a plastic cup
 filled with change.

He sings, head thrown back,
 and rattles the cup so that the coins
 dance like dry seeds in a gourd.

I can't make out his beggar's song,
 but as I pass in front of the windows
 of Marshall Field's I see the mannequins

are dressed up in Ralph Lauren's summer finest.
Two young men pose in one window as if
 they just came from a regatta—they will have

a drink at the club before changing into
 something fresh for the evening —
 it is an image of totally realized youth in cotton.

Next to the mute proportion of their pink limbs
 I see the blind man shaking his
 coins and rattling to heaven as a reflection

in the glass—the afternoon sun bending light
 so that fashion and reality are overlaid
 in a dialectic of poverty and pastels.

Ramon Fernandez, tell me if you know,
is it only in considered reflections
of the rich that life comes to fulfillment,

what of the rest who labor and languish,
what do you make of their rattle and dance?
I am one who is suspicious

of all those who lounge secure
in the inheritance of their wealth,
the blind, who play all day,

and are well dressed, healthy, free.
Has it come to this simple materialism,
was it always so in every empire,

where a young man and his friend,
shirts wrinkled from salt and sailing,
cheeks ruddy from the wind,

are ready to relax, "Look into my eyes,"
one says to another, "They are content and clear—
but wait, what is that rattle we hear?"

Icehouse

Every winter, blocks of ice
are quarried from the frozen river
and dragged by sledges to the icehouse.
They rest on straw in the dark to release,
months later, their cool memory,
to mediate August with a cold radiance.

Eight o'clock in the morning —
the city shuffles out of a tropical sleep.
Below the street, subway trains,
like steel rivers, give up their cargo.
People come yawning into the light,
to melt like ice before the candle of age
or the chlorine hands of commerce.

I owned a house once—as I walk
the humid city I think of its white frame
against a row of wire trees.
I wanted to remain there listening
to the melody of my companion.
Like blocks of ice stored from the river,
my memory gives up those years.
Take what you need for the heat.

Coda

My mother lies dying.
Sleep obscures her eyes like clouds
as her frail heart teeters on the brink.
Light calls her up, while bones
call her back, and between them,
a low music haunts the room.
The balance will tip by a tear.

Once there was this chance and that.
Now there are no more chances.
Somewhere, a girl holds a comb,
and closes the door of her dim room.
Somewhere, a boy whistles,
while rain taps a leaf, and here,
at dusk, my mother lies dying.

It is expected, the braking of water
and flesh—there is no other way.
Yet I say a rare music comes out
when our bones are broken.
This melody is all we can stand.
Listen, do you hear the breath sigh?
Outside, a rustle, and the hinge replies.

Marble Statues of a Kouros

First they stand like transfixed Egyptians.
Years later, the arms come loose from the sides,
eventually they strike a pose just like life.

It is odd, how a whole race can develop over time
as if in technique they were one man alone,
learning to hammer wonders from stone.

The hunger we have for human beauty started
in the blue Aegean, a young athlete in three-
quarter relief, another with the mound of his

organ rising through a rendition of gauze,
lasting the centuries, youth and manhood intact,
the delicate curls of hair chiseled with joy,

this is what we yearn for as children of original
sin, this is the perfection we remember
from the garden, the pool, the tree of life.

It makes one contemplate how the flow of time
fleshes things out, how a human type blooms
and fades, but in its progress to decay, hints

at an end to time and a radiant beauty to come.
Even a stone torso broken seems partially alive,
and because the human form is so ingrained

in our being, it has the weight of whisper,
and suggests another substance could also be
given in time, one in which we may find glory.

To prove it, go sit before a statue of the Buddha —
serene as cool blue light, granite gathering gravity—
now what do you want—I choose the Greek.

Summer Threnody

For Carol Kyros Walker

Flies are knocking against the white siding
of the house with dents of determination.
Zinnias platform themselves to the light.

Pastelled like candy, they invite the bees.
Vines are winding up the strings I tied —
the line of certainty between dark and light

is as strong as the precision of chrome.
It is summer in the sun.
My eyes follow shades of curved surfaces,

metal clamps, the corner of a screen, the edge
of the roof to a point where a bird sits,
and then the emptiness of cerulean sky.

Caught in a trance I fall to the slope
of the bristled lawn, a hedge of flowers,
I look back in my mind across the year and see

what endures, what was accomplished in light,
I lie back with a slow breath and somehow
know that even the long-gone Greeks come down

from the city to swim in a grotto of clear
mountain water, where it falls from a ledge
of smooth stones between tall trees, a grotto

overhung with cool branches to shadow
a pool against diamonds of sunlight,
against the playfulness of splashes,

rolling off our skin, stringing our hair,
even this, imagined from a book, in my small
yard on the edge of a great city, vaporous

on the Illinois plains, even this hints
with an insistence like the flies against
siding, that the first sting of beauty

aims in the right direction, but like all
that begins with flesh, it must painfully
rub abrupt against time, moving the mass

of basalt that makes affection, moving
to an accomplishment of a more subtle
breath, a more refined conception of heart.

Here it is possible that only the old know
how to love, here is life in its middle pause,
flushed with remains of youth, remembering

the first time the glory of a particular body
was naked in bright afternoon, mistaking
what is lent for what is owned, platformed

as it was to the light, begging to look
how the shadows give grace to all the curves
of our distinguished mold, mistaking to touch

a beauty that burns before it heals,
and reading how, after so much is burnt,
there resides in our adventure a greater desire,

a circling sign of smoke, as if suspended
in the summer air, involving winter with a kiss,
but joining too our separate hemispheres.

Pawn Shop

At the pawn shop there is a carousel
of mirrors—all day it turns
with bartered wedding rings that tell
of those who could not make it last.

They come here to sell their wish
for cash—dusty stereos, blues
guitars, old Elgins—dials yellowish —
we wonder if they work.

And those rings, laid out flat,
with bright rhinestones or diamonds
revolving on a dusty, purple mat
or propped in boxes aghast like clams —

whose story do they tell to the old
man with a microscope for an eye,
that keeps this storehouse of odds
and ends next to Jack's Rock and Rye?

Does he look deep into the soul's morass
as he looks into gems, then calls out
a price, or the dreaded word, "Glass,"
or does he just focus on the cut,

comment, with a nod, on how our hearts
would be better off made from stone.
He knows all the tricks with mirrors.
You could live like him, alone.

Imagined, While in Traffic, A Cold Spring

His friends from college all live properly
anchored lives, mortgaged, gifted
with generation; only he sends out, regularly,
change of address cards.

It's a long story, why relationships fail —
there are probably as many books on Hamlet
as there are excuses for his checkered trail.
Like a widow, he offers a studied pose,

and travels from season into decade —
traveling much, he sees much, and yet keeps
the faith ... he doesn't call home to evade
a spouse or plot like actors on the TV soaps —

no one misses him at night.
Does it make sense to blame, to insist
that because of a singular appetite
he saw something in the fabric of the world —

a fire or a chill—he doesn't know exactly,
but it concerns the soul's aspiration
beyond the evident, and he cannot abstractly
dismiss the weight of that vision.

Admittedly, it still remains his burden,
his antique, gilded bird and cage,
hauled from one neighborhood to another,
and though he tries to set it down with age,

though he tries to set it down with words,
it remains a sore around which
the revolving world adheres, as if an itch
of dry leaves, dusty snow, radical clouds, all

found their source of gravity in that moment —
if it were not for that loss, he'd have no crown,
if it were not for the nameless, he couldn't
call by name the rare power in a noun,

or consider splendid his gift attendant,
that enables him to pause with traffic,
and notice the red stoplight, vivid, pendant,
like a wet ruby on the sky's soft throat.

The Melons

For Jeanne Inness

The melons and apples she brought back
from the Kansas farm are in paper bags
that rest in the shadows of the porch.
No complacencies of the peignoir here.

One ripe melon, chilled and sliced,
smiles on a blue plate, ready for breakfast.
It could be the moon of September
floating on a quivering field of stars.

"Wouldn't it be nice to share this,"
she thinks, as she sorts her memories
to the hum of the city—here is moonlight
cut and captured on a plate,

dew on the tiles, the distant xylophone
of birds, a bite of pulp sweet as a kiss.
Some say the bright melon of the moon
is a lover who never catches the sun.

Young Sophocles Leading the Victory
Chorus after Salamis

Another group bussed to the art museum.
Some boys from high school, on tour,
dressed like punk rockers—so bored, they
discretely roll a penny across the floor.

The guards are helpless against their palmed
laughter and well-placed luck.
The bronze by Donoghue, of young Sophocles,
must therefore hold the frozen chord he struck,

and wait for its vibrations to ripple
across two thousand years of ether, he must keep
his fig leaf poised with convention,
and hope his notes penetrate high school sleep.

"Art helps us remember," Sophocles sings,
"Helps us remember the act, the act
of commemoration, the act of making."
But when you are young, what is there

to remember—a penny for your thoughts —
not your actions, but Hollywood's make-believe,
not the old war cry, "Make it new,"
but the commercial, "Make it ugly."

What draws me so to this sculpture
of Sophocles is that he has no costume,
his voice is his only lure.
Unlike the devotees of Kali we see

at art schools—those monks and hacks
who are the last in a line of desperate
Puritans—this naked Sophocles
has a firm buttocks, long fingers,

and lips almost moist from syllables.
Actually, if truth be known,
our young devotees of the crude
descend from those same uncouth

fanatics who dressed in black and banned
plays, dancing, saints, wine,
relics, you name it—our new puritans
have banished beauty, plot, rhyme —

penny-ante antics, their pleasure is not
in singing but in noise, their power
is not in balance but in butchery,
their urge is toward our injury.

Behold the beast, the empty, dark
vowel that stuffs the dumb mouth
of every bronze, the metal remark,
that only naked beauty can mask,

that only art can explain.
Let the barbarians wage war
with their patched jackets, chains,
guitars, or the penny they rudely

left on this bronze poet's tongue.
In their jest, they pretend as priests
to give copper communion
to what they care for least.

At best, they will return to quarantine,
and maybe sometime learn that flesh
disciplined by light is of a finer sheen
than any bronze from lost antiquity.

Illusions

For Alexander Brown

I rehearse the motion of that mutual
divorce slowly in my mind,
and mark each frame as a ritual,
or natural gesture of decline.

Are these illusions of the mind's reply
just millimeters of endurance,
a trick of self, the way the eye
is tricked by flashing photographs?

Maybe my memory is fooled by seasons
too, and the slow fall of leaves is
nothing but the world's brittle reasons,
discovered damp on lowland walks.

Maybe we are tricked by an illusion
of the brass sun as it moves from a high
heartbeat to display bald trees
standing as arteries against the sky.

If so, then so be it, worn to verdigris
by this display as I was by marriage
and tokens from the pastures of peace,
let the trees be bald in a moment

or a month, let my memories ordain
to fall too, piece by leafy piece,
back to their heart, vein by vein,
like bare maples on a black hill.

Essentially naked and prepared,
let the old attempts at schemes
turn brown and wrinkled in the grass,
let the small, saw-tooth dreams

of seduction grind to clay spines.
I would stand stripped of my blanket,
framed in desert light, while inclines
of the last illusion draw juice

from the mouth of essential fire,
that leads from root to branch to bud.
It is within the logic of desire
that all who love will be as new again,

yet meantime wait as outlines on the sky,
that stand, row by wire row,
as roosts for birds to occupy,
then disappear like smoke or snow.

North By the River

We walk down Michigan Avenue
on a December night—slow shoppers
huddled arm in arm below the midnight blue
in bundled coats and scarves of breath.

The Wrigley Building lights shoot thick
beams of gloss across the river,
they glaze with frost a wall of brick—
the bridge wavers with traffic.

A soft snow falls to the collected light
as couples stroll by windows,
stop, point out a sparkling of foil,
then look up to the snow, as it bows

from darkness into light, white dots
descending, as if the world were not right
side up, but these notes were pulled
from a dark well by the draw of light,

as if these flakes were letters of a poem
assembling negative upon a page,
or cotton coming down to mend
a blanket for the night, making our age

forget its business, its separation,
the Siberian expanse of avenues,
this snow, frozen ration from the river
Lethe, falling on the city like dust

upon a memory, syllables of snow
sifted from the sky, that warrant
messengers from white to indigo—
a new world tender with the old.

The Velvet Cord

It is heartrending, these red
maples, these yellow elms.
I feel them united with the sky,
tearing at my blood, cutting hard
with autumn's rusted rituals.

Look, with a gust of wind
the trees are made more bald.
With a gust of wind we turn
to this place of seasonal pain,
to a place where black velvet trees
stand magnet in the hazel air.
I can't take my eyes off them.

I recall now a glass pendant
my mother showed me once.
It was heart-shaped, like a leaf,
and hung upon a velvet cord, black
velvet, like the bark on balding trees.
It had a natural flaw too,
an air bubble at the center.
This made it rare and held
as any empty place the autumn sky.

Mother said it was a gift,
from a doctor, before he left

for China, never to come back.
That rusted autumn she worked
in a dime store, rode the red
streetcar home to her sister's,
the streetcar with yellow cane seats.
That autumn the balding trees
wailed their arms against the sky.

Each autumn pains
as many hearts as leaves.
Some are flawed glass,
or empty like a bubble of air.
Some are maple red by burning,
or dangle from a velvet cord.
Others are off wandering, falling,
drifting down and far with the wind.
One gone as this I call father.

How We Live

Solitary among the smell of smoke and sardines—
warm in terrycloth as the tap water breaks like crystal
over his hands that hold the smell of a woman—

who would believe that once these two were as close
as wrestlers in the dark, who would guess
that palm trees and blizzards would end it all.

If you would dare have dinner here,
and look out from the high windows to rain
and railroad tracks, I would just ask once,
"It did happen, didn't it?"

then something—perhaps an angle of God—
stirred the water and the ripples or the rain,
sent you your way and me, mine.
But it did happen, there is evidence.

Why We Don't Have a Statue of Goethe in the Corner Park

I've not yet been to Frankfurt am Main,
but I see from the poster in the travel agency
window that the opera house there is a namesake
and decorated as sumptuous as a wedding cake.

Here in my city the tall building across from
the travel agency is all smooth steel and glass—
rising forty-five stories. I live in the new
world—this skyscraper is the resultant view

of democracy, while in Europe they still retain
some semblance of nobility and grace. The sons
of immigrants built my city—what kinds
of politics and poetry went through their minds

high above the street—yet not high enough
to see someone waving across the ocean?
O opera of humanity—as millions walk by
cranes hoist more metal to the sky.

Parting

For Scott

After much drinking
we walk home in the small rain.
See how everything shines
in the cellophane night.
Now we admit, half surprised,
we have the same desire.

This may be our last meeting.
I am drawn thin
by giving too much away.
Like water, I fear
my skin vaporizes into rain,
dissolves into mist.

If no one holds us
we evaporate.
This is not a dream
but true to the strike of my bones.
I guess you are breaking apart
drop by drop too.

If Nature Puts a Burden On A Man By Making Him Different, It Also Gives Him Power

I take the days and drill them into beads,
then take the beads and string them leather
and gut into a band of river blue.
Iron Shell will wear this on his heart.
I take red like the late October leaves,
black from the lash of wet branches,
white like the pith of pine wood.
With the power of a widow's loneliness,
certain as the stars on autumn nights,
I number patiently the long year's sorrow,
bead and knot the notes of victory.

Smoke and sun are balanced in the sky.
The wild fruit falls into baskets
and buffalo are fat and furred for winter.
Slowly I weave the shining hours of glass
with rhubarb of meat and peppercorns.
I watch the white light widen on the river
and thirst with the prairie grass gone brown.
Alone at night, beneath the bone moon,
I move past the tents where the warriors sleep.
There I leave these beads of many days.
My power to love is Iron Shell's shield.

Sunset at the Cloister

The clouds are boiling across the sky.
A shaft of light bursts through the arch.
For a moment the evening sun is level
with the pastures of wishing and despair.
By the window her flesh is transformed:
the white shawl, her gold band, the beads,
her whole frame is amber in immortal glow.
"My hands are still young," she thinks,
while all the world is paralyzed by light.

Now she takes hold of her loneliness
and sees the time and place allotted it.
A certain dot of peace seizes her heart:
certitude intervenes between the doubts.
She cannot ask to have God bend his will,
nor would He temper hers to love Him more.
For a moment the evening sun is bright
upon the pastures of simplicity.
The ordinary stands transfixed by light.

Flower Festival at Genzano

In 1761 Süssmilich ... published a work called Götliche Ordnung in which he bade us meditate upon the Divine foresight by which the growth of trees has been stopped least they should inconvenience mankind by pushing their branches into the sky!

—*Herbert L. Stewert*

1.

I decide to cut down the bushes
that shore the lawn against the road.
Salt and snow from last winter
killed the weaker ones
and left only branches
to scrape the sky like bony fingers.
Last night I dreamt of the massacres
in Lebanon and saw the arms of the dead
sticking out of piled rubble
just like the branches
that line my little monastic plot.
Their fingers were curling
in spasms of death, scraping the air.
When I woke I decided to confront
a row of hedges with the determination
of an undertaker, as one who would
rid the living of the dead.
"It's like cutting off fingernails or hair,"
I say, and with my saw and shovel,
rake and gloves, with morning
before me, I begin.
Much is hidden in the earth.
Spiders, strange gray bugs
helpless on their backs, surprised ants;
and deep by the dead roots, grubs
with their white, mucous bodies wrapped
in a sleep that does not suspect.
"We only live on the surface," I think,
as I dig and tug at the forked roots,
smelling the mold and powdered shells

of the life that came before; I the surgeon,
the terrorist bomber, the gardener, nodding
to the mailman, sweating in the cool
autumn air, sawing, hacking, resolving
to get them out like a loose tooth or a scab.

Done. I smooth the ground,
bring some marigolds from the yard
and transplant them on the flat,
gray earth as a bracelet
to hide the scars, something new
to hold a space left by the dead.
It cost me though, this working the earth.
I will dream of the dead wood trimmed
like long, red nails, fingers and twigs
rattling in the air, the arms of the dead
shrinking to bone and mushroom dust,
it cost me, with calluses on both hands too.

2.
Did you know the cedars of Lebanon grow
tall and straight like the pines of Portugal?
If Providence did not mean for men to cut
down those trees we wouldn't have built
ships to cross the sea, ships with tall
masts that made America, if they didn't
cut down those trees we wouldn't be here
in this brave new world of Coke and stereo,
with topless towers on the shores of Michigan.
Yet could we not propose to ask what grace
it is that likewise rains bombs on Lebanon,
turns the tress of Portugal to ships,
promises to lift the limbs
of those long dead to dance?
What direction makes marigolds bloom
here as bracelets for the earth?
The sharp, clean smell of marigolds,
antiseptic balm that rubs my memories
of childhood, reverting to fallen leaves,

listening to the el trains scream
their slicing wheels down the length
of a Chicago alley; marigolds on father's grave,
grandson to a Jewess from Hamburg,
come here alone to open a saloon
on Halsted Street.
What direction allows memories
to dance in the autumn light
with an unstudied amplitude,
like the grace of those leaps
some dancers know,
held for a moment,
yet destined to fall, and by falling
made most beautiful, and by falling
to suffer the pains of Lebanon,
the pines of Portugal,
arms reaching out
from Germany to Illinois,
reaching out with arms of flesh,
joint to bone, bone to heart,
heart to limbs, strong limbs
to dust, and from the dust
another seed, another dance.

3.
The truth is, I wanted those dead
bushes out and the house in shape
because the ballet is coming to the college
where I teach, and some of the dancers
will be staying with me.
I know one of the boys from New York
and wrote him when they danced here last.
He didn't answer, but that's probably
because I sent along some suspicious poems.
You may question the motives of art,
wonder at the purpose of formality in dance,
but once I saw this man dance and was taken
outside myself with the gentle power
of his movements, his arms and legs poised

as if the power of the resurrection
lived in them, as if the dead limbs
and branches of our ancestors
were lightsome flesh, as if bombed
cities re-assembled themselves
like a movie run backwards.
I wanted to dance like that too
and to be held close in the warmth
of such a moving, manly power.
I never told this to Keith, but as I hack
the arms off dead bushes,
dig up their feet, shake clotted earth
off their veins and toes, their roots
that search the darkness, and perhaps
by some design are tied to my hair —
so when I pull I am also pushed—
as I do this I recall the dreams
of wasted lives, as I do this work
of earth I am made so mortal
I beg our bones be quick again,
beg that Ezekiel was not wrong.
As I crack a knuckle of wood,
the way a lamb's leg is cracked,
to show a pearl socket rimmed
with pink flesh like the lips of a shell,
I know we need delight in dance again
and skirt among the reeds like sparks.

Letter to Brainsure —
Being a Translation of the Spanglish
Original—Dated 2378

"It was a hard and wonder-struck journey,
but we bring back treasures for all.
Since coming here from Wide River Station,
four have died—sores, hairless,
yellow puke and moan—one, a blond
girl of seven, we buried yesterday.
The legend is true of concrete and caves.
Many strange things we found—
marvelous suits and hoods of metal cloth.
The giants who built these worship-cones
probably wore those hoods in alien rites,
before the days of global suns.
We have found signs in gringo speech too.
Look to the old books, ask the guardians
what they mean, who remembers why,
reactor rods arranged in spider dust,
drums that read 'Nuclear Waste' gone to rust."

St. Joseph's Church, Stratford

Water from the river tumbles
Through the lock's cement controls.
A wind mixes in the willow boughs
And the metal of the high bells toll.

They come in polished cars
For a wedding on the hill.
Across the sprinkled lawns they stroll,
Through blooms of daffodils.

Will you tell them, St. Joseph—
Who was kept from Mary
By the plan of God—
How each bell slap carries
Judgment too across the pools,
Tell them of the terrible rule
That necessitates a separate few,

A few who celebrate outside today,
Recalling those who turned away,
Or those, who brought their love
Through treks of snow,

To stand before the altar's glow
And pray, "Please give me this,"
But find the empty years insist
God's answer has been "No."

Security

Look at that house
with blistered siding—
the sun hammering it
for years, and wind too,
with a thousand
whips of rain—

two-by-fours and plaster,
a tar-paper roof against
the white stare of stars—
look at that balloon,
floating above neat
needles of grass.

Exhibit Hall

At the museum we study an oriental lacquer
bowl colored red with cinnabar—it holds
only air now, free from wars and empires.

I recall how Adam keeps Jeff's ashes in an urn,
on the dining room table—those bits
of bone that were once a complete desire
rest in the red hollow of a brass embrace.

Mixed up at the end, the virus in his brain,
Jeff asked for a "book of pills, a glass of mink."
Eventually the tongue trips over itself.

Downstairs, a dinosaur skeleton, assembled
like a troublesome puzzle, chews at the air.
Who else sees the terrible angel of victory
that surrounds this architecture of bones?

I watch Phil looking up at the open ribcage,
a battlefield of ash at his feet—I touch his
hand, tell him, 'The war's over, let's go home."

Birthday Song

Holy Milton, blind and broken, I suffer
heat too, and cannot write the way I would
if all were well in me. The golden grapes
of youth are stale, a musty smell of yeast
is on my breath. I wait. Will grace distill
a vintage from my work or just a cask of vinegar?

A book can only be a pause, a lull within
the din of war. A book is where the author is,
wrestling with the trinity of what is now,
and what will be and what has come before.

I am in body come of age. I am in soul
still in a cage. I write the words I know,
and listen to a voice that speaks with dreams—
O singing from the stars, O chorus tuned from worms,
your notes and pulse resound—I feel I am
still rising up, while falling under ground.

Planting Tulips

*The last and best cure of love melancholy
is to let them have their desire.*

—*Robert Burton*

After a parade of beauties,
each one more beautiful than the other,
he is asked to choose.
"I love best the one I saw last,"
he answers, and so ends the dream—
a dream from sleep in the afternoon,
on the sofa, curled with a small pillow.
The sun has warmed the front room,
and with the gauze curtains filtering the light,
the coffee table roses are dark silhouettes
of detailed stems and thorns
disappearing into a milk glass vase.
They are adolescent now, another day or two
and they dip their heads like old women.
The calculation that it is late,
almost time for supper, comes over him
like the diminishing of a drug.
Getting up, sitting on the sofa's edge,
toes searching for slippers,
a familiar noise from the street somehow
reminds him how small the world seemed
as a child, how going around the block
on his bike was an adventure for a week,
and then the newspaper route, more of the city,
and college, followed by years of traveling,
years of foreign food, politics,
the second civil war over long hair
and Vietnam, it all makes childhood
seem a point on a vast map, an outpost
on an unfinished draft, something suspended
in the rare state between sleep and action.

Will thirty years from now do the same
to that force born of flesh, that force
that sends fingers rubbing after thighs
like misers rubbing old money, will thirty years
see his glandular motives shrunk to a point
of insignificance, and the one image
that blinds him since junior year,
that one wish, be but a provincial dot,
buried in the ordinary soils of experience,
buried as the tulips which went in this morning,
early, while the ground was soft after
an October rain, too early, so he sleeps
this afternoon, rare tulips, screwed in slits
of earth, covered from the wind and snow
of winter, waiting, planted with the mystery
of all seeds, the primordial wonder
of what happens in the dark,
what happens as we move away in time.
Or will it be like the bird he saw flap
from one pole to another across the sky,
settling on point after point of dipping wires,
moving away like an ancient nomad to work
other pastures, and then return following
spring to find the soil lit up with flowers,
lit up with tulips tossing their heads,
each one more beautiful than the other,
tulips kissing the sky, tulips,
once secreted, now tunneling upwards,
wax red and succulent, local,
yet on axis with the sun, red tulips,
pressing like their two lips.

The Sun Catcher

I propose a place with waterbirds, a low country
of marsh and reeds, with waves lapping against
sandy islands of dune grass, the sky spotted
with the white pebbles of clouds.
I propose a sheltered inlet, a cove, where the blue
leakage of the sea undulates like water in a bowl.
Here, growing out of the beach, on stilts
of gray wood, a house of many rooms unfolds.

In one of those rooms, a high bed relaxes
after the pressure of sleep, springs back
like the grass after so many steps. Here, too,
is a table with potted plants on embroidered cloths—
one large philodendron tosses its tangled leaves
like his hair, when he stepped from the water,
lit from behind by the sun, as translucent and sacred
as glass that floats upon the liquid walls of Chartres.

I propose a stillness of heart that forgives time's
scourge of memory, that opens to the moment where
I see him on that bed and remember how my body
was one white tooth, that ached for the taste of his body,
and so he gave, and I took, the way glass or leaves
take the light that passes through them from a low land
of waterbirds, thrown out like a weave of limbs,
or the victory of words wrestled from the world.

The Vanishing Theater of Regards

She asks me if I still love him. "Yes, I do,"
I say, "but it's different now, he doesn't
Live here anymore—since we were in school,
He's moved to Florida and forgetfulness."

All our particulars are bled away and just
A shell remains—it is as if an auditorium
Were imagined evaporating, metal gone to rust,
The gilded hall, full orchestra, silk screens,

Breastplates and battlements, hum by hum
Diminish; violins, trumpets, tambourines,
All fade away, there is a dampening of drums,
The curtain turns to threads, melodies dim,

All that remains is a song without words,
The bright, magnetic music of a seraphim —
As radiant as the high, cold, light April leaves,
Luminous behind these almost greening trees.